• Learning Connections •

W9-ATF-778

Colonial America

Complete Theme Unit Developed in Cooperation With The Colonial Williamsburg Foundation

By Mary Kay Carson

SCHOLASTIC
PROFESSIONAL BOOKS

New York 🐚 Toronto 🐚 London 🐚 Auckland 🐚 Sydney 🐚 Mexico City 🐚 New Delhi 🐚 Hong Kong

ACKNOWLEDGMENTS

The author wishes to thank The Colonial Williamsburg Foundation of Williamsburg, Virginia, for its cooperation on this project. Special thanks to the Foundation's Suzanne Coffman of the Publications Department for providing a plethora of resources and endless assistance, and to School and Group Service's Elizabeth Maurer, tour-guide extraordinaire.

Contents

About The Colonial Williamsburg Foundation

Williamsburg was founded in 1699 as the capital of England's large and prosperous Virginia colony. As the capital, it was home to the British royal governor, the colony's legislature, and the high courts. Lawyers, merchants, and people from all over the colony came to Williamsburg to do business in this important and busy town.

During the years leading up to the American Revolution, Virginia legislators traveled to Williamsburg to discuss and debate the path to independence. Many of these legislators, such as George Washington, Thomas Jefferson, and Patrick Henry, helped lead the 13 colonies to nationhood.

In 1780, Virginia's capital was moved to Richmond. Williamsburg settled into a quiet existence until 1926, when John D. Rockefeller, Jr., agreed to restore the town to its Revolutionary-era appearance. Today, Colonial Williamsburg is the oldest and largest living history museum in the world. More than one million people visit it each year.

A visit to Colonial Williamsburg's Historic Area is a journey back in time. More than five hundred buildings, including the Capitol and the Governor's Palace, have been restored or reconstructed to their eighteenth-century appearance. Artisans in shops demonstrate their trades for the public, and costumed interpreters interact with visitors, discussing eighteenth-century ideas and issues. Horse-drawn wagons and carriages roll down the streets, and oxen, sheep, and poultry inhabit pastures and pens. The Historic Area changes continually as ongoing historical and archaeological research alters our understanding of America's colonial past.

The Colonial Williamsburg Foundation worked with Scholastic Professional Books to develop this book, providing lesson plans, primary source materials, research, and illustrations to the author and the editors at Scholastic. Colonial Williamsburg historians, tradespeople, and curators reviewed the text and illustrations. It is our hope that the lessons and resources in this book will enable teachers to bring the colonial era and Colonial Williamsburg to life in the classroom so that, in the words of John D. Rockefeller, Jr., "the future may learn from the past."

Pete Pitard
Director of School and Group Services
The Colonial Williamsburg Foundation

Colonial America at Work

In the Beginning...

An estimated 500,000 Native Americans lived along the eastern seaboard when European settlers began arriving in North America. In the north lived the Abenaki, Wampanoag, and Pequot nations as well as other groups. The future "middle colonies" were home to the Delaware (or Lenape), Susquehannock, and Iroquois nations. Tribes to the south included the Catawba, Cherokee, and Powhatan. These nations had their own languages and traditions, yet they shared a few things in common. Most lived in villages where they grew corn, squash, and beans. Some tribes were semi-nomadic, farming and fishing in villages during the summer and moving to forest hunting grounds during the winter.

Native Americans introduced European settlers to skills that would revolutionize their lives. They taught the newcomers about the native plant, corn, which would become a staple of colonial life not just because its kernels fed people and chickens, but because its husks filled mattresses, its stalks fed cattle, and its cobs could be made into everything from tools to dolls. Native Americans also taught Europeans about valuable resources like *hickory* trees and *squash* plants, and animals like *raccoons*. These and many other words we use today are rooted in Native American languages.

Above: An engraving of a Native American published in 1590.
Right: An early map of Virginia from the 1600s.

Native American populations plummeted in colonial times as English settlements grew and diseases brought from Europe ravaged villages. As settlers traded and fought with Indians, the Indians' way of life changed. Some tribes banded together to fight the settlers or sought alliances with England's enemies—especially France. Others entered into the British economy by trading furs and hides, selling baskets or other crafts, or working as day laborers for the colonists.

Defining "Colonial America"

England was not the only European player in the high-stakes game of establishing colonies in North America. By 1607, when Jamestown was founded, a Spanish settlement already existed in present-day New Mexico. To the south, the Spanish town of Santo Domingo, in what is now the Dominican Republic, was celebrating its 111th birthday. The busy harbor of Havana, founded 88 years before Jamestown, served as the dispatch point for Spain's huge fleet of galleons that returned home each year loaded with Mexican treasures. Spain clearly

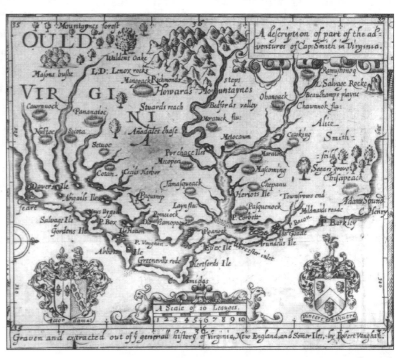

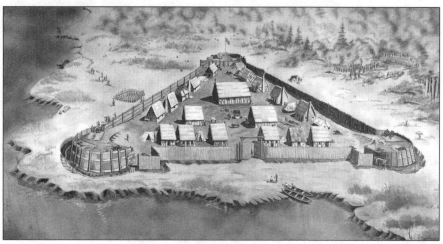

had established its own version of "colonial America" by the time the English arrived on the scene.

At the same time England was expanding its colonial presence in North America, so too were France, the Netherlands, and other countries. While the town of Williamsburg was growing as a center of colonial Virginia politics, for example, French settlers were busy building outposts at present-day Biloxi, Mississippi, and New Orleans; Spanish missionaries were creating missions in California; and the explorer Vitus Bering was claiming Alaska for Russia.

What life was like in colonial America, then, depended on where and when you lived. This book focuses on what everyday life was like for people who lived in the 13 English colonies that later became the core of the United States.

An artist's conception of the Jamestown settlement, the first permanent English colony in America.

Who Came to the 13 Colonies?

Most of the 13 colonies' earliest settlers came from England, Scotland, Wales, and Ireland. Those who went to Virginia and the southern colonies were mostly young, single men who hoped to strike it rich or at least own their own piece of land. By contrast, many early settlers in Massachusetts were English families seeking religious freedom as well as a new start in life. Like the young men headed south, many of these early northern colonists knew little about farming or even hunting, two of the skills most needed in colonial America. Many came from towns and cities rather than farms and made their living as tradesmen or common laborers. Few had any experience with hunting because only gen-

tlemen could own guns in England, and game belonged to the owner of the land where it ranged. By the time of the Revolution, however, the majority of colonist were farmers, and ownership of guns was widespread.

The "middle colonies" of New York, New Jersey, Pennsylvania, and Delaware attracted the most diverse group of settlers. Families streamed in from places like Germany, the Netherlands, Sweden, France, and Switzerland for religious freedom as well as new economic opportunities. One German settler described the boat that brought him to Pennsylvania as a "Noah's ark" of religious beliefs since it held Roman Catholics, Lutherans, Quakers, Mennonites, and others.

Because it was expensive to travel to and start new lives in the colonies, many of the early European settlers came to the 13 colonies as indentured servants. In exchange for four to seven years of hard work, indentured servants received their passage to America as well as a bare minimum of clothes, tools and, sometimes, land of their

1492
Columbus lands in the "New World" and claims it all for Spain.

1565
St. Augustine, Florida, is founded by Spain. It's the first permanent European settlement in the present-day United States.

1585
English settlers attempt unsuccessfully to establish a colony on Roanoke; a fourth group arrives two years later, only to disappear and become the "Lost Colony."

1607
The first permanent English colony in America is founded at Jamestown.

own. As the 1600s and 1700s progressed, the number of indentured servants arriving in America diminished, the overall nature of immigration to the colonies changed. America's growing towns and cities attracted educated and skilled individuals who could pay their own way and who provided needed services. Many of these later immigrants were merchants, physicians, and skilled tradesmen.

By the late 1600s, people throughout the colonies were also depending increasingly on a different kind of worker—enslaved peoples originally from Africa. At first, most slaves were put to grueling work in the expanding tobacco fields of the South. But enslaved African Americans could also be found in every colony along the eastern seaboard, doing everything from sewing to shipbuilding. Olaudah Equiano, also known as Gustavus Vassa, was captured in Africa and sold as a slave when he was 11 years old. He worked, among other places, as a slave in the fields of Virginia, aboard an English naval vessel, and in the counting houses of the West Indies and Philadelphia. After he bought his freedom, Equiano traveled the world. He eventually became London's most prominent black abolitionist.

Wherever they lived in colonial America, slaves had few rights, suffered whatever punishment their masters chose to inflict on them, and often endured harsher punishments for crimes than free people. They couldn't own weapons, own real property, assemble together freely except at church, or legally marry. The family life of a slave was cruel and uncertain, since mothers, fathers, and children often were separated from one another when one was sold or hired out to work in faraway fields.

By 1776, about one of every five Americans would be an enslaved African American.

What Did They Bring?

Some of the most powerful things colonists brought with them were their ideas of how life should be lived. The English, for example, brought their views of society as highly stratified, with people belonging to different classes. It's important to remember that the credo "all men are created equal" was a concept foreign to English society at the time. People belonged to four main classes— and a person's clothes and speech instantly gave away where he fit in the English world. The aristocracy were the wealthiest, most educated, and powerful people in England. They dominated the highest government offices. Below them were the gentry. The definition of "gentry" was pretty slippery by the eighteenth century. In previous generations, the right to a coat of arms (as confirmed by the heralds of the College of Arms) had defined gentlemen, but the eighteenth-century definition was broader. If a man had sufficient income (usually from rents and assuredly not from working with his hands), a good family, education, and taste, he probably qualified. Defined this way, the gentry class included large landholders, some physicians, some barristers, some clergy, and some merchants who dealt in overseas trade. Members of the gentry could serve in the House of Commons and were usually the local justices of the peace. Below the gentry were the "middling sort," a larger group of civil servants, tradesmen, retailers, lesser doctors and lawyers, and small farmers. They lived comfortably, worked for a living, and held minor offices. Under them were the vast majority of English, the "lower sort." These day laborers, tenant farmers, small-time tradespeople, and sailors had no political rights in England and could be forced to work in mines, serve in the army or

1616
A smallpox epidemic nearly wipes out all the Native Americans living along the New England coast.

1619
The first Africans are brought to mainland North America as indentured servants.

1620
The Pilgrims land in Massachusetts and sign the Mayflower Compact.

1651
The Navigation Act requires that all colonial imports and exports be shipped in English vessels.

1692
The Salem witch trials take place in Massachusetts.

navy, or be jailed for being out of work at any time. People who worked hard and prospered could move up in society, however.

In the colonies, these levels were compressed. There were very few aristocrats (mostly royal governors), and the colonial gentry usually did not correspond to the top English gentry. American gentry held the highest political offices and led the colonies, while gentry women supervised servants, entertained guests, and saw to the education of their children. Most white colonists were of the "middling" sort. Most middling men were farmers, small planters, or tradesmen. Middling women often worked in family shops or at skilled trades to contribute to their families' incomes, while men and women of the "lower sort" labored as indentured servants, tenant farmers, or day laborers. Because land was plentiful, upward mobility was viewed as a distinct possibility.

Other traditions transplanted to the colonies from Europe were more concrete. Swedes introduced a form of home architecture that was used in Sweden and Finland—the log cabin. Dutch builders popularized porch additions to houses that they called "stoops." Germans contributed two innovations that would revolutionize pioneer life—the highly accurate frontier rifle and the roomy Conestoga wagon. Germans and Swedes also introduced the soon-to-be-quintessentially American traditions of house- and barn raisings. Africans made major contributions to American culture as well. For example, the banjo and "southern" foods such as okra, yams, and black-eyed peas all have roots in African cultures. Enslaved Africans also contributed their expertise in cultivating rice—a crop commonly grown in parts of Africa—thereby making possible a new, lucrative industry in the southern colonies.

Student Activities

🏛 A Map of the Past

All 13 original colonies eventually became states. However, their boundaries changed much during the years before statehood. In this map-reading activity, students compare and contrast the early borders of the colonies with current state boundaries.

Materials

A Map of the Past (page 16), The 13 Colonies, Then and Now (page 17), a United States map

Here's How

1. Divide students into pairs. Challenge the class to name the original 13 colonies. Write their answers on the board.

2. Distribute a copy of A Map of the Past; The 13 Colonies, Then and Now; and a United States map to each pair of students. Have them check and correct, if necessary, the names listed on the board. Then have them complete The 13 Colonies, Then and Now.

3. Lead a discussion of the answers. Then expand the discussion to how this exercise has affected students' understanding of the 13 colonies and how they changed in subsequent years.

Answers to The 13 Colonies, Then and Now: 1. Virginia; Georgia; 125 years **2.** France **3.** Maine is no longer part of Massachussetts; New Hampshire is smaller **4.** Southern; bigger as colonies **5.** Appalachian Mountains **6.** Choctaw Indians **7.** West Virginia; Kentucky **8.** Approximately 70,000 square miles; multiplied length by width

EXTENSION ACTIVITY

Challenge partners to make a set of overlay maps, using transparencies, that show how colonial America changed over time. Some students may

1763
The Treaty of Paris ends the French and Indian War and cedes some French lands in America to Britain.

1765–67
The Stamp and Townshend acts levy duties and taxes on many imported goods and official documents.

1770
The Boston Massacre leaves five colonists dead at the hands of British soldiers.

1773
The Boston Tea Party occurs in December, causing Britain to close Boston Harbor in 1774.

1774
The First Continental Congress meets in Philadelphia.

▶▶▶

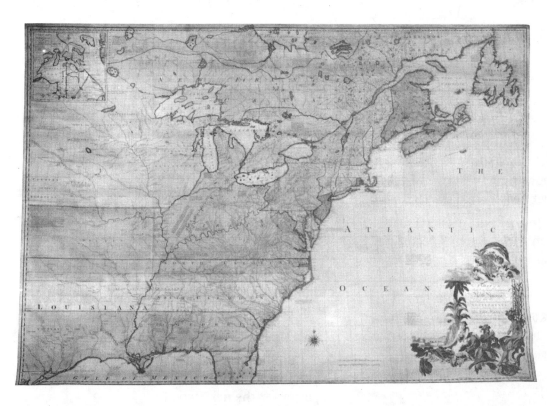

A map of the British colonies completed by John Mitchell.

want to contrast who lived in eastern North America before Europeans arrived with who lived there in 1776. Others may want to highlight patterns of settlement by colonists. Students will need to consult encyclopedias or historical atlases for this activity.

 ## Signs of the Times

In this activity, students become acquainted with the diversity of occupations that contributed to life in colonial America, as well the way colonists put art to practical use.

Like today, shops and businesses were essential to life in colonial America. Almost no one was self-sufficient, not even farmers. The majority of the population depended to some extent on nearby tradesmen and merchants for goods and services.

Colonial shops and businesses had bright signs outside them, just as stores do today. Often the signs had pictures or symbols of the trade or merchandise that could be found inside. Those who couldn't read would be able to tell what kind of business it was just by a sign's symbols. The pictures also served as advertising. (This adapted from The Colonial Williamsburg Foundation's Teaching Unit, *Signs of the Times*.)

Materials
Signs of the Times (page 18), markers or crayons, paper

Here's How
1. Divide the class into small groups for this warm-up exercise on the concept of interdependence. Challenge groups to brainstorm a list of items they use or eat every day. Compile a general list

1775	1776	1781	1783	1784
The first battles of the American Revolution are fought.	The Declaration of Independence is adopted.	British forces surrender at Yorktown, Virginia.	U.S. and British representatives sign a peace treaty in Paris, officially ending the Revolutionary War.	Congress ratifies the peace treaty.

from the groups on the board. Then expand the list into a chart with the following categories: Who made the items? What went into making them (materials, skills)? Where did they come from (store, foreign country)? Could students make the things themselves? Encourage students to guess intelligently whenever they're not sure of an answer. Have students draw conclusions about how things we use and need connect us with other people.

2. Shift the discussion to the context of colonial times. Remind students that colonial people had no WalMarts or other huge, all-purpose stores. If you broke your rifle, for example, a gunsmith would have to forge new parts for you—there were no such things as standard, ready-made parts. Challenge student groups to brainstorm a list of things colonists would have needed in everyday life and how or where they might have acquired these things.

3. Now hand out a copy of Signs of the Times to each group and have them complete the exercises. Have volunteers share their original sign designs with the class.

Answers to Signs of the Times: shoemaker, apothecary, gunsmith, tailor, tavern, wigmaker

Williamsburg: A Colonial Capital

The poster of Colonial Williamsburg will help students visualize the layout and dynamics of a real colonial town. It will also help root the people and places mentioned in this book in their actual geographic contexts. Consider making the poster the center of a bulletin board display that includes the following question cards.

Materials
Poster (bound in book), 2 pockets for question cards, bulletin board, Q & A on Colonial Williamsburg (page 19), blank index cards cut to the size of the other question cards

Here's How
1. Set up the poster and card pockets on the bulletin board. Leave plenty of space around the poster for the next activity.

2. Cut out the question cards from Q & A on Colonial Williamsburg and place them in one pocket. Put the blank cards in the other pocket. Label each appropriately.

3. During available times, have small groups of students go to the board to scan the poster and answer questions. Encourage students to work together to come to a consensus on answers. Also challenge students to write questions of their own on blank cards for other groups to answer. Students should sign their names to the backs of cards they contribute.

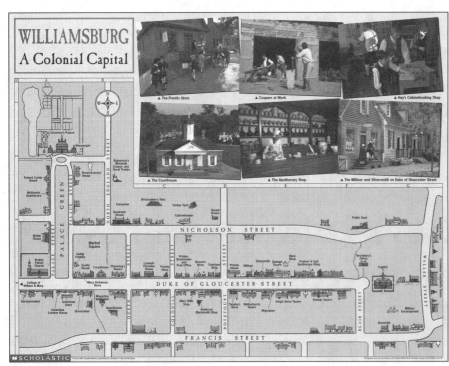

 People of Williamsburg

Students can meet some of the people who lived in Colonial Williamsburg with the People of Williamsburg cards, which highlight the lives of real people who lived in Virginia's colonial capital during the 1700s.

Materials

People of Williamsburg (pages 19–21)

Here's How

The cards can be used in many ways throughout your unit.

- Cut out the profile cards. Divide the class into ten groups and give each group a card. Each group's job, first, is to link their person to a specific place on the Williamsburg poster—the place where he or she lived, worked, and so on. Later, they can pin their card to the bulletin board and mark the spot where their person lived or worked with a pushpin and yarn leading to their card. In the meantime, groups should brainstorm topics to research that will shed more light on how their person lived from day to day. (The group with Clementina Rind, for example, might want to explore what went into printing a colonial paper and what it looked like.) Groups can then decide on the most vivid presentation format for their report, such as a written report, a video presentation, or a song.

- Another option is to have students choose a person from the cards and write a "Day in the Life of . . ." story or play about him or her after they have done additional research about life in colonial America.

- Have students assume the character of one of the people featured on the cards, then be interviewed by the class. Encourage students to do additional research that will add richness as well as authenticity to the person's profile (for example, if she ran a tavern, find out what colonial taverns looked like, what they served, and so on).

- As you continue with other activities, refer to these ordinary people whenever possible to provide context. For example, when doing Reading the News (page 45), refer to the newspaper publisher Clementina Rind, whose paper you will be reading.

 Stitching a Book

In colonial times, bookbinders made each volume by hand, stitching the pages together with heavy thread and covering each volume with a handmade cover. It took apprentices several years to master the skills involved in this process. One skill they learned was how to make beautifully colored papers that served as endpapers in some books and covers in others. In this activity, students practice the basic techniques used to bind books as well as make eye-catching covers. (Adapted from an activity by Sandi Yoder published in The Colonial Williamsburg Foundation's *The Apprentice*.)

Materials

¼ cup flour, 1¼ cups water, saucepan, stove, whisk, 1–2 tablespoons powdered tempera paint, white 8½-inch by 11-inch paper, 2- to 3-inch paintbrush, blank paper, waxed paper, wide-toothed combs or plastic forks, string or yarn, hole punch, white glue (optional)

Here's How

1. Combine the flour and water in the pan and heat to boiling, whisking constantly. Remove the pan from heat. (NOTE: Take appropriate caution if you will be completing these first two steps with students.)

2. Stir in the powdered paint and set aside to cool. (To use more than one color to decorate the covers, repeat steps 1 and 2 with different colored paint.)

3. Place sheets of white paper on a table. (You may want to protect the table with newspaper.)

4. Brush a thin layer of the colored paste all over the sheets of paper (or brush stripes of different colors).

5. Have students use a comb or fork sparingly to create swirling designs in the paste.

6. Let the papers dry completely. These will be the book covers.

7. To make the inside pages, fold paper in half to make 5½-inch by 8½-inch sheets. Have each student prepare several sheets of paper.

8. Punch three holes along the folded edge of each sheet, making sure that all the holes are aligned.

9. Cut a 2-foot-long piece of string or yarn. Push the string down through the center hole, leaving a 3-inch tail. Then thread the string up through the top hole, down through the center hole again, and up through the bottom hole. Tie a knot near the center hole.

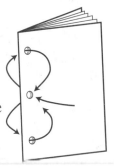

10. Prepare another batch of paste, as in step 1, or simply use white glue to paste the covers onto the front and back pages of the book. Sandwich a sheet of waxed paper between the inside cover and front page and the back page and back cover to keep them from sticking together while drying. Place each book inside a folded sheet of waxed paper and stack weights on top of the books to flatten them. Let the books dry.

11. Discuss with students what this process taught them about colonial books and bookbinding.

EXTENSION ACTIVITY

Encourage students to use their creations for a book about some aspect of life in colonial America—colonial fashions, famous and not-so-famous people, colonial jobs, and so on. They can also use it as a journal to document what they learn about colonial America.

Casting Marbles

Expert metalworkers were essential to colonial life. Smiths hammered metal into shape. They made and repaired goods from silver bowls (silversmiths) to hoes (blacksmiths). Founders cast brass, pewter, and other metals into the candlesticks, spoons, buttons, musket balls, and other objects colonists needed. Much of their work was done in foundries, where ovens known as forges heated metals to melting points of over 2,000°F. Founders first made intricate molds out of sand. Then they poured molten metal into them. (Customers sometimes brought worn-out metal goods to be melted down and "recycled," because most metals weren't yet being mined in America and it was illegal to import unworked metals into the colonies.) After the metal cooled and hardened, the molds were broken and the spoon, candlestick, or button filed and polished. Students experience a bit of what it took to be a good founder in this activity using soap molds to cast plaster of paris marbles. (In colonial times, marbles were made by hand, but we've made adaptations for this activity.)

A founder at work at the Geddy Foundry.

Materials

Bath-size bars of soap (1 per student), serrated bread knife **(for adult use only)**, plastic spoons, craft sticks, rubber bands, plaster of paris, water, measuring cup, plastic container, funnel, emery boards, paint, brushes

Here's How

1. Before class, carefully cut the soap bars in half with a bread knife.

2. Give each student 2 half bars of soap, a spoon, and craft stick.

3. Have students use the craft stick to plane smooth two of the broad sides of the soap bars, as shown.

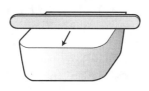

4. Next, have students draw a quarter-sized circle on one side of each soap half. Tell students they want to create a mirror image, so the circles need to be at the same height.

5. With a spoon, carve out a hemisphere on each circle.

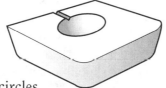

6. Carve a straw-sized channel down to the circles.

7. Place the soap halves together and rubber-band them securely, being careful not to obstruct the channel's opening.

8. Mix the plaster of paris according to the package directions. (It's usually 2 parts plaster to 1 part water.)

9. Fill each mold with plaster of paris using the funnel. (You may want to protect the table with newspaper.) Let them dry overnight. **NOTE: Don't pour plaster of Paris down the drain—it will clog!**

10. Open the molds and snap off the rod-shaped sprue from the channel. Students can sand their marbles smooth with emery boards and paint them.

11. Encourage students to share what this activity has taught them regarding colonial foundry workers and what skills they needed.

EXTENSION ACTIVITY

Help students play a colonial era marble game with their marbles. On a flat dirt surface, dig a few holes that are big enough to trap a marble. A short distance away, draw a line in the ground. This is the line behind which "shooters" must stand. Have teams of students compete to toss their marbles into the holes on a single round, or encourage students to make up their own games. (Note: This game was originally played among individuals, not teams, but since students only have one marble apiece, it's being recast as a team event.)

The Doctor Is In: Colonial Medicine

Formally trained physicians were rare in most parts of colonial America. Rural colonists relied primarily on home remedies and folk cures to treat illnesses and medical problems, and midwives delivered most babies. (Some doctors also delivered babies; they were called man midwives.) In towns, apothecaries (pharmacists) often practiced as doctors and prescribed, made, and sold treatments to customers. Some treatments—like using leeches to "bloodlet" a patient—were ideas brought from Europe. Many of the plants and chemicals that apothecaries used to prepare medicines were also imported, although a few, such as snake root and sassafras, were found locally. In this activity, students learn about eighteenth-century medical treatments.

Materials

The Doctor Is In (page 22), scissors, glue or paste

Here's How

1. Ask students what their families do for them when they have a cold. Do they offer any home remedies, like chicken soup, honey with lemon, or flat ginger ale? Explain that during colonial times, people relied on their own knowledge or perhaps that of a local apothecary to treat ailments, because physicians were few and far between.

2. Distribute copies of The Doctor Is In. Have students cut out the treatment cards on the

Inside the Pasteur & Galt Apothecary Shop in Colonial Williamsburg.

bottom of the page and attempt to match the cures with the ailments—without pasting at this point. Then have students work in groups to compare and rethink answers, then glue the cards into place.

3. Go over the answers with students. Elicit their thoughts on each cure: Why do you think they thought that? Would it work? Would you want to try it? What would we use today?

Answers to The Doctor Is In: 1. C **2.** E **3.** D **4.** G **5.** H **6.** A **7.** F **8.** B

Sign Me Up!

During colonial times many 14- to 21-year-olds lived and worked with skilled tradespeople in order to learn a trade. They were called apprentices. Boys apprenticed with printers, smiths, coopers, apothecaries, and tailors; girls mostly apprenticed for household work or in trades typically performed by women, such as millinery and laundry. How long people served as apprentices depended on how old they were when they started their apprenticeship and what trade they were learning. The tradesperson usually taught the apprentice the craft and basic reading and writing. (In some colonies, the law required masters to educate their

apprentices.) Arithmetic was also important to help keep the books. In exchange, the apprentice was expected to work hard and contribute to the tradesperson's shop—and sometimes even pay a fee for the privilege of learning! Some apprentices lived in the master's home and were given food and clothing. A good apprenticeship could decide the success of a young person's future, and apprenticeships were legal contracts drawn up between the master and the apprentice's parents (or the church, if the apprentice was an orphan). Students fill out an original apprenticeship contract in this activity and debate the pros and cons of such an arrangement.

Materials
Sign Me Up! (page 23)

Here's How

1. Discuss with students how people today learn a skill like plumbing or computer repair. How do they think people learned skills 300 years ago? Have students brainstorm a list of skilled colonial trades they have been introduced to through activities and profiles of real people who lived and worked in Colonial Williamsburg (smith, bookbinder, cooper, and so on). Introduce the idea of an apprenticeship to students.

2. Distribute a copy of Sign Me Up! to each student. Read the contract as a class, helping students understand the language. Check for understanding by asking questions such as: *What did the master agree to do? What did the apprentice agree to do? What was the apprentice forbidden to do?*

3. Challenge students to choose a colonial trade that they think would have been interesting to learn. (If they are having trouble remembering some of the choices available, show them copies of Signs of the Times, page 18.) Then have students work to fill in their contracts, having chosen a trade to "apprentice" in.

EXTENSION ACTIVITY
Challenge students to research the trades or skills they chose. How long did apprentices have to work to master their trades? What kinds of skills did they

A wheelwright at work.

learn during their apprenticeship? If possible, have students draw a captioned flowchart that shows the different manufacturing steps involved in their trades.

Colonial Coins and Prices

Money was a problem in colonial America—there simply wasn't enough of it to go around. Colonists weren't supposed to mint money, nor were they allowed to import money from England. What were they to do? Many began using commodities such as tobacco and foreign currency to buy and sell goods. Spanish pieces of eight circulated alongside English shillings, Dutch guldens, and Mexican milled dollars. A coin's value was usually determined by its true weight in silver or gold, not its face value. Merchants would think nothing of taking a foreign coin from a customer, then weighing and cutting it to make change. In this activity, students compare the relative worth of currency used in the colonies, plus their purchasing power. (Note: the values of coins shown are based on 1766 rates.)

Materials
Colonial Coins (page 24), Colonial Prices (page 25)

Here's How
1. Divide the class into pairs. Distribute a copy of Colonial Coins and Colonial Prices to each pair.

Have them complete the activities in Colonial Coins first, after which they can move on to the next sheet. Help students work out problems on the board as necessary.

2. Discuss what the problems taught students about the colonial economy (relative value of goods, and so on).

3. Encourage partners to write story problems of their own using the data from the two worksheets. Have pairs exchange problems or hold a "Math-Bowl" competition using their own problems.

Answers to Colonial Coins: 1. shilling; half 3 gulden; half crown; milled dollar; 2 escudos, Louis d'or; half Joe **2.** the bigger, the more value **3.** 20 **4.** 3 **5.** 12 **6.** 10 **7.** 5 **8.** $\frac{2}{3}$

Answers to Colonial Prices: 1. 2; 1 shilling **2.** breeches **3.** 60 **4.** Answers will vary. **5.** 880

EXTENSION ACTIVITY
Have students set up a colonial store, complete with products marked with accurate prices and a cash box stocked with cutouts of colonial coins. (You may want to back the coins with poster board and have students color the coins gold or silver.) Students can shop at the store or work behind the counter.

A Map of the Past

In 1750, a British mapmaker named John Mitchell took on the challenge of mapping Britain's colonies in North America. It was a huge task that had been tried only once before in the 1700s. The map on this page is based on Mitchell's work. In what areas do more than one group of people claim to control land?

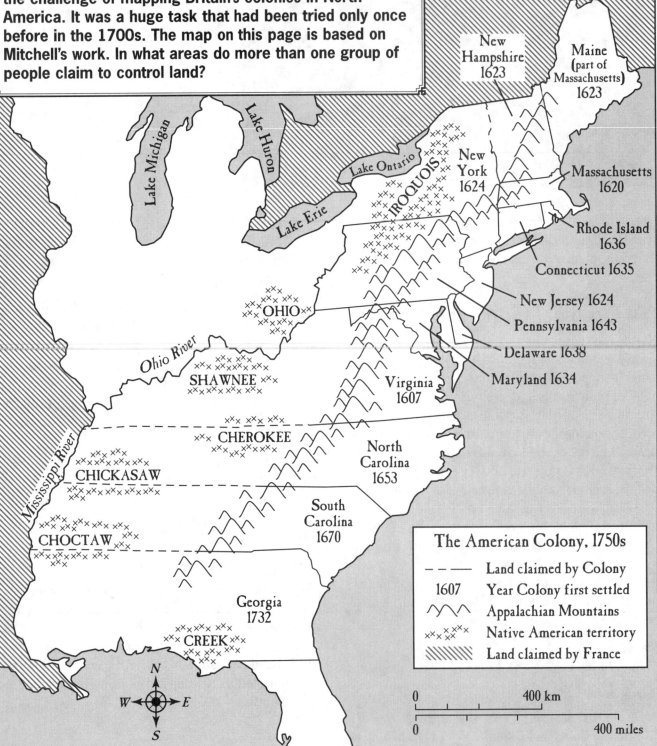

New Hampshire 1623

Maine (part of Massachusetts) 1623

Lake Michigan

Lake Huron

Lake Ontario

Lake Erie

IROQUOIS

New York 1624

Massachusetts 1620

Rhode Island 1636

Connecticut 1635

New Jersey 1624

Pennsylvania 1643

Delaware 1638

Maryland 1634

OHIO

Ohio River

SHAWNEE

Virginia 1607

CHEROKEE

North Carolina 1653

CHICKASAW

Mississippi River

South Carolina 1670

CHOCTAW

Georgia 1732

CREEK

N W E S

The American Colony, 1750s

– – –	Land claimed by Colony
1607	Year Colony first settled
⌃⌃⌃	Appalachian Mountains
×✕×✕×	Native American territory
╱╱╱	Land claimed by France

0   400 km

0   400 miles

Colonial America   Scholastic Professional Books

The 13 Colonies, Then and Now

**You'll need a modern-day map of the United States
plus A Map of the Past to solve these problems.**

1. Which American colony was settled first by Europeans? Last? How many years passed between the

first and second date? _____

_____

2. Who claimed the land to the west of the Mississippi River? _____

_____

3. How has Maine changed since its colonial days? New Hampshire?_____

_____

_____

4. Which colonies changed more before becoming states, the northern or southern colonies?

Explain your answer. _____

_____

_____

5. Which mountain range separated colonists from many Native American nations? _____

6. Who lived in the western part of the land claimed by the colony of Georgia? _____

_____

7. Which states now make up land once claimed by the colony of Virginia?_____

_____

8. Estimate the area of land claimed by North Carolina in the 1750s. Explain how you got your answer.

_____

_____

_____

Signs of the Times

Colonists depended on expert workers like the ones listed below to meet their basic needs, and shop owners did all they could to attract customers. These picture signs from Colonial Williamsburg served two purposes—they advertised their shops, and they described what the shops were to people who couldn't read. See if you can figure out what each sign stood for.

Some Colonial Trades

apothecary: made and sold medicines, and drugs

barber: cut hair, shaved beards, sometimes made wigs

blacksmith: hammered iron into nails, ax heads, door hinges

bookbinder: stitched and bound pages into books

brickmaker: turned clay into bricks

cabinetmaker: made and repaired furniture

chandler: made candles

cooper: made containers like barrels out of wood

gunsmith: made and repaired guns and rifles

milliner: made dresses; sold buttons, ribbon, and imported cloth

printer: hand-printed newspapers and sold books

saddler: made saddles, harnesses, leather water buckets, hoses

shoemaker: made boots and shoes

silversmith: made expensive silverware and jewelry

tailor: custom-made clothes, often of wool

tavern keeper: provided meals, lodging, and entertainment

wheelwright: made wooden wheels for carts and wagons

whitesmith: made iron objects, polished them to look like silver

Now choose five other trades from the list and design eye-catching signs of your own for them.

Colonial America   Scholastic Professional Books

Q & A ON COLONIAL WILLIAMSBURG Use these question cards for your bulletin board display.

Where on the map's grid is Bruton Parish Church located?	What famous building is located in A-1?
What would be the quickest way to get from the Capitol Building to the Governor's Palace?	You need to get from the Public Gaol to the Courthouse. What routes could you take?
How many taverns are there in downtown Williamsburg?	What streets run parallel to Duke of Gloucester Street?
Duke of Gloucester Street was Williamsburg's main street. What important building was at its easternmost end?	You work in the kitchen of the Governor's Palace. Do you work in the actual Palace? In which direction is your workplace from the Palace?
You work at Wythe House (A-3). Your mistress wants you to buy some medicine at an apothecary's shop. How many shops could you go to in town? Which shop is closest to your workplace?	Farmers come to Market Square (B-3) six days a week to sell goods. One of them wants to go to Christina Campbell's Tavern (G-4). How could he get to the tavern from Market Square?
You work as a carpenter building outbuildings at Peyton Randolph's house (B-3). You need more nails from the blacksmith. Where is his shop located?	You're going to add a shed to your house. At which stores might you buy the wood and other supplies you need?

PEOPLE OF WILLIAMSBURG

Jane Vobe—Tavern Keeper

I run the King's Arms Tavern on Duke of Gloucester Street. I've run a tavern since my husband fell off his horse and died 20 years ago. (I'm not the only widow running a tavern—it's quite common, since it's not that different from running a big household.) For those of you who don't know, a tavern is like a hotel. Travelers can stay overnight in rooms, and there's a bar and restaurant too. I have 18 slaves who buy food at market, cook, and clean. I supervise them and try to keep all my guests happy from sunup to sundown. I can read and write, and I keep track of all the money that changes hands here. As a widow, I can own property, but I can't vote.

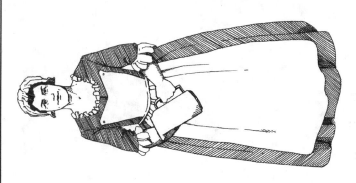

Clementina Rind—Printer

My five children and I live near the Prentis Store on Duke of Gloucester Street. I'm 33 years old and run a busy printing business out of our house. I edit a newspaper, the *Virginia Gazette*, and also print documents for the House of Burgesses— the lower house of Virginia's legislature. No other woman in the colony has ever run a business like mine. The reason I got into this business is sad, though. My husband, William, was a printer, but when he died this year (1773) I had no choice but to take over.

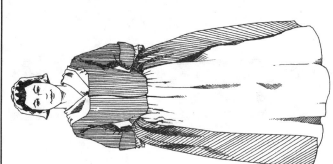

Anne Blair—Gentlewoman

My father, brother, and I live on Duke of Gloucester Street, right near the College of William and Mary. My granduncle started the college in the colonies. My father served as Virginia's acting governor for a while.

I'm 23, not married yet, and one of my favorite things to do is to go to balls and dance. This summer I've also got something else to do, though. My ten-year-old niece, Betsey, has come to stay with us, and it's up to me to supervise her reading, sewing, and dancing lessons. (The minuet dance is our favorite!) Betsey must know how to behave as a young lady should. It's very important in this day and age.

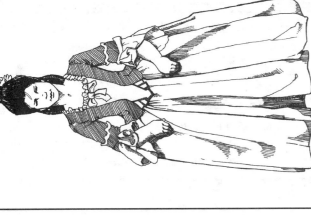

Anthony Hay—Cabinetmaker

I've made some of the best furniture in the colonies at my shop on Nicholson Street. We've also repaired fine furniture and harpsichords and other musical instruments—things that you'd find in only the best homes. (A number of cabinetmakers and apprentices have worked for me, even a carver who just arrived from London.) I never expected to do quite this well! But I'm giving up the business to start a new career, owning the most popular gathering spot in Williamsburg, the Raleigh Tavern. Thomas Jefferson and George Washington have been customers when they've been in town. So have other well-known gentlemen.

Judith—Slave, Household Cook

In the eyes of the law, I belong to William Prentis, owner of the Prentis Store. I live with my children, Molly and Tom, at the Prentis house on the corner of Duke of Gloucester and Botetourt. We live above the kitchen, where I work as the family cook. (The kitchen is a separate building from the rest of the house.) Every day I get up before dawn to make the Prentises' breakfast. Then I get started on dinner, the midday meal that's the biggest meal of the day. In between meals, I work in the household garden and pick up the food I need at market. My daughter goes to a school for slaves—she learns to read the Bible there. But there's talk that Molly might be sent away soon to work for someone else. I won't be able to bear it if the Prentises do that to us!

[NOTE: The future did bring separation to the family. Molly remained with the Prentis family, but Judith and her son Tom were sold at auction. We don't know who bought them. If Judith and Tom's new masters lived in town, the family was probably able to see each other. If not, they might have run away for short periods to visit each other, as many slaves did.]

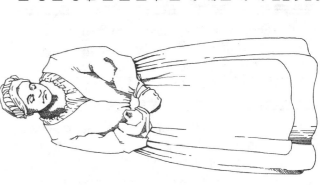

William Prentis—Merchant

I'm one of the biggest merchants in town. My store, on the corner of Duke of Gloucester and Colonial, sells paper, books, fabric, hats, shoes, sugar, tea, tools, and other goods from England as well as Virginia. I grew up a poor orphan in England. At 14, I apprenticed myself to a merchant here, and in exchange for the passage over, I worked seven long years. That taught me all about the business, though, and in time I bought the store myself. Now I've got a wife and eight children, and slaves to attend to us in our big house just down the street from the store. Besides running the store (with the help of my sons and a nephew), I loan money to customers or let some buy things on credit. I'm also a Justice for James City County, which is no small responsibility.

Adam Waterford—Free Man, Cooper

Americans of African descent like me make up about half of this town's population. Most are slaves, though. (That includes my wife. Someday I hope to have enough money to buy her freedom. If I don't, any children we have would be considered the property of her master! By law, children born to slave women are considered slaves.) I'm not a slave. I'm a free man. I own my own place on the southeast edge of town (though I still can't vote, even though I own property), and I make my living as a cooper. That means I make all kinds of containers out of wood—buckets, barrels, tubs, butter churns. It's not easy turning a bunch of straight boards into curved, watertight containers! You need to know a lot about wood and metal (since we use metal rings to hold the boards together).

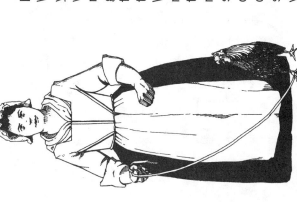

Martha Cripps—Farmer

I live about an hour's cart ride outside of Williamsburg on a farm. My husband died a few years ago, so my four children and I have to work hard to keep the farm running. We couldn't manage without our slaves, Sam and Bess. We grow tobacco, corn, and other vegetables and fruit and raise cows so we can sell milk and butter. I get up well before dawn so I can drive to Williamsburg and sell our products at the big market on Market Square. Most customers get there at around daybreak, so I've got to hurry! By midmorning nobody's buying anything anymore, so I pack up my things and come home. Then I do laundry, mend clothes, weed the garden, check up on Sam's work in the fields. (My oldest son works with Sam out in the fields, while my younger ones help me around the house.)

Peter Pelham—Musician, Jail Keeper

I was born in England but moved to America as a child. I studied music in Boston and have been the church organist at Bruton Parish Church. But like most musicians, I have to work another job to pay all my bills. Since I'm married and have many children, I've got even more reasons than most to work hard! I am the colony's jail keeper. People are jailed because they're waiting to go on trial or owe money; runaway slaves who've been caught are also held until their owners come to claim them. But people aren't put in jail as "punishment." (Our idea of punishment runs more along the lines of public whippings or death by hanging.) It's my job to feed the prisoners every day. I also check to make sure their chains are securely fastened. (Some are chained within their cells.)

James—Slave Gardener

In the eyes of the law, I'm owned by the Burwell family of Carter's Grove plantation, eight miles outside of Williamsburg. But the Burwells have rented me out to work at the Governor's Palace here in Williamsburg because I'm needed for my special gardening skills. (The Burwells make 12 pounds a year from this deal.) I know how to get plants to grow out of season, and I can prune fruit trees and transplant hard-to-grow seedlings. I learned these skills from the governor's head gardener. Each Saturday evening, I "night-walk" the eight miles home to my wife, Betty, and family at Carter's Grove, so we can spend Sundays together. I'm proud of my 15-year-old son, Juba, who's learning to make barrels from the head cooper at Carter's Grove. My girls, Phebee (age 13) and Jenny (8), are also a great help to their mother.

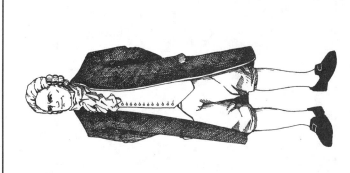

The Doctor Is In

Because physicians were rare in colonial America, people depended on home remedies and apothecaries for treatments. Cut out the treatment cards at the bottom of the page. Then match the treatments with the ailments below. Check with your teacher for the answers. You might be surprised! When you've got them right, paste them on.

My boy cut himself with a knife.

I need to brush my teeth.

My husband has a swollen arm.

Eek! We have lice.

1.

2.

3.

4.

I've trouble with acid stomach.

My daughter sprained her ankle.

The boys are sunburned.

My oldest girl is throwing up.

5.

6.

7.

8.

A	B	C	D
apply a pack of clay mixed with strong vinegar	place a halved onion on the stomach	clean with turpentine	drain blood with leeches
E	**F**	**G**	**H**
clean with frayed roots of licorice tree	rub with buttermilk	rub tobacco snuff into the scalp	take lozenges of chalk

Colonial America   Scholastic Professional Books

Sign Me Up!

Back in colonial days, teenagers were part of the workforce. Many youths signed up to learn a trade such as metalworking, bookmaking, or sewing from an expert from the time they were about 14 years old. From that moment on, they were no longer kids but full-fledged workers called apprentices. If you had to sign a real-life document like this, what trade would you want to learn? What would be some pros and cons of signing up?

This indenture states that _____, with the permission of
NAME OF APPRENTICE
his parents, does of his own free will put himself apprentice to learn the

_____ art, trade and mystery, and, after the manner of an
NAME OF TRADE

apprentice, to serve from the day of _____, to the full end
START DATE

and term of _____.
END DATE

During this whole time the apprentice will faithfully serve his master, keep his secrets, and readily obey his every command.

- He will not waste his master's goods, nor lend them unlawfully to anyone.
- He will not get married within the term.
- He shall not play cards, dice or any other unlawful games.
- He shall neither buy nor sell his own goods nor the goods of others without permission from the master.
- He shall not leave day or night from his master's service without the master's permission.
- He shall not haunt ale house, tavern or play-house, but in all things behave himself as a faithful apprentice ought to do.

The master shall do his best to teach and instruct the said apprentice in the

trade and mystery of _____ and prepare and provide for him
NAME OF TRADE

meat, drink, lodging and washing, fitting for an apprentice during the said time.

_____
SIGNATURE OF APPRENTICE AND PARENTS

_____
SIGNATURE OF MASTER

In witness whereof the said parties have set their hands and seals hereupon dated

the _____ Day of _____ in the Year
DATE   MONTH

of our Lord One Thousand Seven Hundred and Eighty-two.

Colonial Coins

British Money
20 shillings = 1 pound

The colonists didn't have their own coins. They used coins from all over the world. How did colonists know how much the foreign coins were worth? It depended on how much silver or gold they contained. Coins were weighed and assigned a certain value based on British money. Merchants thought nothing of cutting up coins to make change! As you'll see as you answer the following problems, colonists had to be good at math to make sure they weren't cheated when out shopping!

1. Number the coins from the least valuable (1) to the most valuable (7).

2. How did the size of coins affect their value? _____
_____

3. How many shillings was a Spanish 2 escudos worth? _____

4. How many Dutch half 3 guldens did it take to equal 2 British half crowns? _____

5. You want to buy something that costs 3 pounds. How many Mexican milled dollars will you need to buy it?
_____

6. You want to exchange a French Louis d'or for its worth in Dutch half 3 guldens. How many should you get?
_____

7. A customer buys something from your shop that costs 1 pound, 5 shillings and pays with a Brazilian half Joe. How much change in British half crowns should you give her?
_____

8. You pay for a 1-shilling handkerchief with a British half crown. The merchant has run out of change but can cut the coin into pieces to give you back what he owes you. What fraction of the coin do you think he needs to give back?
_____

Silver British shilling
(worth 1 shilling)

Gold French Louis d'or
(worth 1 pound)

Silver Dutch half 3 gulden
(worth 2 shillings)

Mexican milled dollar
(worth 5 shillings)

British half crown
(worth 3 shillings)

Gold Spanish 2 escudos
(worth 1 pound)

Gold Brazilian half Joe
(worth 2 pounds)

Colonial America   Scholastic Professional Books

(The value of the coins has been rounded up and down.)

Colonial Prices

A little bit of money went a long way in colonial America. Check out what you could have bought or sold with the coins in Colonial Coins.

1. How many whole bushels of apples can you buy with a Mexican milled dollar? How much change should you get back?

_____

_____

_____

2. What's cheaper to buy, a wig or 4 pairs of breeches?

_____

_____

3. How many pounds of cornmeal could you buy with the amount you'd pay for a pound of tea?

_____

_____

4. You have a French Louis d'or to spend at the store. What would you buy? How much change would you have left over, if any?

_____

_____

_____

_____

5. How many pounds of bacon could you buy with the amount it would cost to buy a round-trip ticket to England?

_____

British Money

12 pence = 1 shilling
20 shillings = 1 pound

(The value of the coin has been rounded off.)

Prices in Virginia, 1770

Eggs (1 doz.) . . . . 6 pence
Apples (1 bushel) . . . . 2 shillings
Sugar (1 lb.) . . . . 8 pence
Coffee (1 lb.) . . . . 1 shilling
Tea (1 lb.) . . . . 10 shillings
Chocolate (1 lb.) . . . . 3 shillings
Bacon (1 lb.) . . . . 6 pence
Chicken (1 whole) . . . . 6 pence
Oranges (1 doz.) . . . . 3 shillings
Turkey (1 whole) . . . . 2 shillings
Cornmeal (1 lb.) . . . . 2 pence
Breeches (pants) . . . . 7 shillings
Handkerchief . . . . 1 shilling
Cap . . . . 4 shillings
Wig . . . . 2 pounds
Petticoat . . . . 10 shillings
Hammer . . . . 2 shillings
Pencil . . . . 3 pence
Table . . . . 2 pounds
Round-trip to England . . . 22 pounds

Manners and Morals, Law and Government

"Manners Maketh Man"

The Englishman William of Wykeham declared in about 1400, "Manners maketh man." Well over 200 years later, that saying continued to be the motto ruling many colonists' lives. It's hard for us to imagine, in our modern era, how structured life in colonial America was. Especially in the early colonial period, hierarchy and rank pervaded every aspect of life—clothing, occupation, hobbies, speech. Even something so simple as greetings between two people reflected social divisions. In the 1600s and early 1700s, only gentlemen, for example, could be called "Esquire" or "Master" (which in ordinary speech became "Mister"), and gentlewomen, "Mistress" or "Mrs." Ordinary men were known as "Goodman," and ordinary women, "Goodwife" or "Goody." By the time of the Revolution, respectable middling people were called "Mister," "Miss," or "Missus."

Because society was so stratified, it was important that everyone behave according to his or her rank in life. This was one reason why mastering proper manners was so important to wealthy and well-educated colonial families—it simply wouldn't do to act uncouthly and thereby drag down the family's place in society. One Virginia aristocrat vowed, for example, that his children would "better be never born than ill-bred."

Many well-bred parents relied on a slew of etiquette books to reinforce the manners their children were learning. (Rules included maxims, like "Never speak to thy parents without some title of respect, as *sir, madam*, & c." and "Spit not, cough not, nor blow thy nose at the table, if it may be avoided.") Parents of all ranks also quoted Bible verses, old English proverbs, and even Aesop's fables to reinforce principles of wise and respectful behavior. Anywhere and anyplace, it seemed, there was a "moral of the story" that could be told.

Laws and Government

People living in the British colonies were British subjects beholden to the king, but each colony had its own governor, a legislature of some kind, and a court system. In general, at least one house of government in each colony was elected by eligible colonists. This meant, for the most part, white males who owned a certain amount of property (though there were rare cases of some free African Americans voting in southern colonies until the 1720s). Colonial legislators debated issues, levied taxes, and passed laws for their colony. However, the legislatures were beholden to the British government, which could, and did, reject laws it considered not in accordance with British laws. Because most colonial government positions paid no salary and, moreover, because only landowners voted, most elected officials in the colonies were male members of the gentry.

Styles of government at the local level varied greatly among the colonies. New England's famous town meetings, for example, elected local officials each year to manage local affairs, while appointed

The House of Burgesses in the Capitol building in Colonial Williamsburg.

A reenactment of a trial at the Courthouse in Colonial Williamsburg.

officials governed local concerns in many other colonies. Sheriffs, constables, local courts, and juries were especially important when it came to the matter of enforcing law and order. Crime certainly didn't pay in colonial times. People convicted of anything from horse-theft to murder faced swift public executions by hanging. Lesser crimes ranging from gossiping to burglary garnered punishments from having to stand gagged in front of one's house to having one's hand branded with the letter "B." Only those on their way to court, some debtors, and captured runaway slaves awaiting return to their masters were held in jails. Colonial jails were means to achieve the end of punishment, not the end itself.

Growth and Revolution

The English colonies grew quickly. At the beginning of the eighteenth century, about 250,000 non-native people lived in the English colonies. By the time the American Revolution started in 1775, there were an estimated 2.5 million people. The colonies not only grew, they prospered—the living standard was soon equal to that of Europe.

Britain's policy toward its American colonies after the French and Indian War precipitated conflicts that ended in revolution. The war ended in 1763 with a defeated France ceding most of its North American holdings to Britain. The colonial armies emerged from these wars with military confidence. The British government emerged with vast new amounts of territory to defend and administer. The British ministry felt that the empire needed stricter administration and that the colonists should help bear the costs incurred by the war. To that end, customs regulations were tightened, stamp duties were applied to documents, and taxes were levied on goods shipped from Britain to the colonists, who couldn't legally import goods from anywhere else. This "taxation without representation" was met with resentment, boycotts, and, in Massachusetts, protests, which led to British soldiers firing upon and killing five members of a hostile crowd in Boston (the Boston Massacre of 1770). Was it in the colonists' best interests to remain affiliated with Britain—the ancestral and cultural home of so many Americans—or to set off on their own independent destiny? This was the crucial question of the mid-1770s, and the debate and actions that ensued would literally revolutionize the colonial world.

Student Activities

Minding Your Manners

In this activity, students gain insight into what was expected of people socially during colonial times. They also become acquainted with the ornate cadence of eighteenth-century English. Colonial children—especially those born into wealthy or well-educated families—were drilled in rules of etiquette from early on. When he was about 15 years old, George Washington practiced his penmanship by writing out a list of social do's and don'ts that had been compiled by an Englishman more than 100 years earlier. His copy, now known by the mouthful title of *George Washington's Rules of Civility and Decent Behaviour In Company and Conversation*, lists 110 rules explaining how gentlemen should behave in public.

Materials
George Washington's Rules of Civility (page 31)

Here's How

1. Distribute a copy of George Washington's Rules of Civility to each student.

2. Allow students time to read over the rules. Then ask them about their general impressions: Were colonial times more strict or less strict? Do you think these rules were for men and women? Do you agree with all the rules? What are some common themes in the rules? *(respect for others, reserve in behavior, and so on)*

3. As a class, go over each rule, making sure that students understand its meaning. Ask students if they know modern equivalent rules. *(Don't talk with your mouth full, and so on)*

4. Divide students into groups and challenge them to write modern translations of the rules. Then have groups write their own top 10 rules for classroom civility.

🏠 Fabled Cards

Aesop's fables were popular reading and teaching materials during colonial times. Some playing card decks even featured illustrated fables alongside the cards' suits and numbers. In this activity, students match the story poems from four of these cards with their morals and interpret their meanings for modern times.

Materials
Fabled Cards (page 32), heavy paper, glue, scissors

Here's How

1. Begin by reminding students that fables are simple stories that teach lessons or morals. Have volunteers summarize fables that they know.

2. Distribute a copy of Fabled Cards to each student. Have students cut out the cards or paste the sheet onto heavy paper and then cut them out. As students cut out the cards, they can match the morals to the fables.

3. Allow students time to read through the cards and ask questions about unfamiliar words. Check understanding of the fables by asking questions, especially about the morals.

4. Divide students into groups and assign each

group a fable. Have each group talk about their fable and write a modern translation of it. Challenge them to come up with a few real-life situations that their moral would apply to.

5. Challenge groups to turn their fable into a mini-play and present it to the class. Have the class guess the moral of each play.

Answers: *The Wolf and Pig:* "Believe not those who often friendship swear…"; *Jupiter (the God) and Camel:* "With whatever Heaven grants you be at rest…"; *The Bear and Two Travelers:* "What was't he whispered in your ear…"; *The Cat and Mice:* "Good counsel's easily given…"

EXTENSION ACTIVITY
Challenge students to find out more about Aesop and his famous fables. Then have them research the sayings of Benjamin Franklin in his *Poor Richard's Almanac.* How were Franklin's sayings similar to the fables of Aesop? Different?

🏠 A Colonial Trial

In this play, students re-create a trial based on real trials that took place in colonial Virginia during the 1700s. The defendant, accused of hog theft, is tried before a panel of justices, then acquitted or convicted by a jury—in this case, the students themselves. Through this activity, students become acquainted with colonial standards of law and order, which are quite different from our own. (Adapted from the Colonial Williamsburg Foundation's Teaching Unit, *Order in the Court.*)

Materials
A Colonial Trial (pages 33–36)

Here's How

1. Reproduce A Colonial Trial and distribute a copy to each student.

2. Review unfamiliar legal terms with students

before beginning *(prosecution, defense, attorney, jury, credible witness).*

3. Decide who will perform the roles in the play. Students can use their own names for the parts, or make up names if they want. The number of justices can vary depending on your class size. Extra students can also portray the courtroom audience. In the eighteenth century, only men would have held the position of Sheriff, Clerk, Deputy King's Attorney, Chief Justice, juror, or justices. The script has been written to reflect this fact. When girls are assigned these parts, the people speaking to them can pretend they are men.

4. Put the case in its geographic context by locating places mentioned in the trial on the Williamsburg map: Courthouse (B-4), Public Gaol (F-3).

5. Invite the class to read and/or act out the play. Stop and check for understanding during the play by asking questions such as: *What are the two sides? Who is in trouble? What did he do? Is she a good witness?*

6. At the end of the play, invite students to debate the merits of each side in the case. See if students can come up with a unanimous verdict, as was required for this case. Tell students that the first time someone was found guilty of hog stealing, he or she could receive up to 25 lashes in a public whipping. A person convicted of hog stealing for a second time would be placed in the pillory with his or her ears nailed to the pillory. After two hours, the person would be freed by having the parts of the ears that were nailed to the pillory cut off. A person convicted a third time faced execution.

7. Encourage students to compare and contrast this case and its punishment with modern court proceedings. How is it different? *(There's more than one judge; the defendant is not entitled to the help of a court-appointed lawyer; the punishment is harsh by today's standards, and so on.)* How is it the same? *(The defendant isn't guilty until found so; witnesses are called to back up each side of the case; witnesses swear to tell the truth, usually on the Bible, before taking the stand, and so on.)*

COLONIAL CRIME AND PUNISHMENT

Colonial ideas about crime and punishment were very severe by today's standards. Indeed, many colonial sentences wouldn't stand up to today's interpretation of the Constitution and its banning of "cruel and unusual punishment." Punishments ranged from the paying of fines to whipping, imprisonment in stocks, and burning on the hand. Not everyone was equal under the law. A free person convicted of stealing a pig, for example, received 25 lashes, whereas a slave or Native American was given 39 lashes. Anyone convicted of a more serious crime like horse stealing, arson, or murder, though, faced death by hanging. These and other punishments were carried out in public places so that everyone, including children, could watch—and be reminded of the dangers of straying from the straight and narrow path of good citizenship.

🏠 Loyalist or Patriot?

As the colonies moved toward independence, people began to take sides on what was best for America. Loyalists believed it was best for the colonies to maintain their ties with Britain, while patriots pressed for freedom from British rule and its taxes. The side a person took depended largely on his or her background, family ties, and occupation. A blacksmith who had no family in England and whose business would increase if war were declared, for example, most likely would be a patriot. A newly arrived millinery shop owner who sold mostly imported goods, by contrast, would likely remain loyal to the king. In this activity, students assume the roles of colonial people and debate their views on the rising prospect of revolution.

Materials

Loyalist or Patriot? (page 37), scissors

Here's How

1. Set the scene for students. It's 1774. The Stamp Act and the Townsend Duties have been repealed, but the colonists still pay a tax on tea. The Bostonians' protest against the tea tax—the Boston Tea Party in December 1773—caused Parliament to close the port of Boston as of June 1, 1774. Parliament also enacted other laws infringing on Massachusetts citizens' traditional rights as Englishmen. People in other colonies are afraid they will lose their rights, too. The First Continental Congress meeting in Philadelphia has just adopted a Continental Association pledging not to trade with Britain. With tension escalating in the colonies, people are taking sides for and against the British government's policies.

2. Introduce the point/counterpoint nature of the loyalist/patriot debate by reading students the poem on this page, Bobbi Katz's "Party Plans." Ask students how it sums up conflicting arguments in the loyalist/patriot debate. Write

their contributions on the board. Then challenge students to research arguments made by colonists for and against independence.

3. Divide students into groups of six. Distribute a copy of Loyalist or Patriot? to each group. Then have groups cut the sheet into its six cards and debate the various points of view represented. Who is a loyalist? A patriot? Who's undecided?

PARTY PLANS
ABIGAIL BERNARD, 1773

My father's in a fury.
    And so are all his friends.
England treats us like we're chattel
    to use for its own ends.
England thinks that we Colonials
    have no right to make choices.
They disregard our envoys.
    English ears can't hear our voices.

Now bankruptcy is facing
    their most precious company.
England wants to save it.
    At what cost?
    Our liberty!
They've cut tea taxes to three pence
    for their own monopoly:
Their chosen few are the ones who sell
    British East Indian tea!

Tea merchants like my father
    can buy fine tea from the Dutch.
We don't need tea from England.
    Thank you very much!

A party's planned in Boston.
    Who's coming?
They'll be many.
    Will there be cups of British tea?
Tea, yes!
    But cups... NOT ANY.

          —*Bobbi Katz*

George Washington's Rules of Civility

When George Washington was about 15 years old, he transcribed a list of rules for behaving properly in colonial society. Here are a few of his rules.

- In the Presence of Others Sing not to yourself with a humming Noise, nor Drum with your Fingers or Feet. (RULE NO. 4)

- Sleep not when others Speak, Sit not when others stand, Speak not when you Should hold your Peace, walk not on when others Stop. (RULE NO. 6)

- Turn not your Back to others especially in Speaking, Jog not the Table or Desk on which Another reads or writes, lean not upon any one. (RULE NO. 14)

- Keep your Nails clean and Short, also your Hands and Teeth Clean yet without Showing any great Concern for them. (RULE NO. 15)

- Show not yourself glad at the Misfortune of another though he were your enemy. (RULE NO. 22)

- Do not laugh too loud or too much at any Public Spectacle. (RULE NO. 24)

- If any one come to Speak to you while you are Sitting Stand up though he be your Inferior. (RULE NO. 28)

- Run not in the Streets, neither go too slowly nor with Mouth open go not Shaking your Arms kick not the earth with your feet, go not upon the Toes, nor in a Dancing fashion. (RULE NO. 53)

- Whisper not in the Company of Others. (RULE NO. 77)

- Speak not Evil of the absent for it is unjust. (RULE NO. 89)

- Being Set at meat Scratch not neither Spit Cough or blow your Nose except there's a Necessity for it. (RULE NO. 90)

- Blow not your broth at Table but Stay till Cools of it Self. (RULE NO. 94)

- Put not your meat to your Mouth with your Knife in your hand neither Spit forth the Stones of any fruit pie upon a Dish nor Cast anything under the table. (RULE NO. 95)

How would these rules sound in "modern" English?
What are your own top 10 rules for classroom civility?

Colonial America   Scholastic Professional Books

Fabled Cards

Colonists loved fables by the ancient Greek storyteller Aesop. They even printed versions of the fables on playing cards, complete with "the moral of the story." See if you can match each story with its moral.

THE WOLF AND PIG ♦

A Wolf urges the Pig that he might be
A guard, to keep her Pigs from Injury.
The Pig, who knows the nature of the Beast,
Replies, "When absent, Sir, you'll guard them best."

JUPITER (THE GOD) AND CAMEL ♥♥

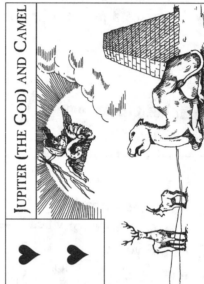

For Horns the Camel Jupiter implored,
With which so many beasts so well were stored.
The god, enraged, replied, "your Forehead wears
Henceforth no Horns and, what is worse, no Ears."

THE CAT AND MICE ♠♠♠♠

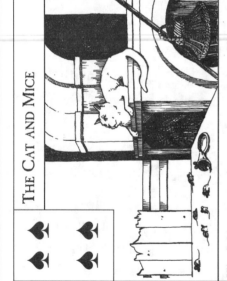

The Mice debate how to prevent their Fate,
By timely notice of the approaching Cat.
"We'll hang a Bell about her Neck," cried one;
A second answers, "Who shall put it on?"

THE BEAR AND TWO TRAVELERS ♣♣♣

A Bear approached two Travelers; one fled
To a safe tree, the other lay still as dead.
The Bear, but smelling to his face, retired:
The friend climbed down and, laughing, thus inquired:

MORAL: With whatever Heaven grants you be at rest, For it knows where to place its Bounty best.	MORAL: Believe not those who often friendship swear, Lest they some private interest should prefer.
MORAL: Good counsel's easily given, but the Effect Oft makes it uneasy to transact.	MORAL: "What was't he whispered in your ear?" asked he; "He told me, 'Shun a treacherous friend like thee.'"

Colonial America   Scholastic Professional Books

A Colonial Trial

Characters:

Narrator (a Court TV–style reporter)

Chief Justice

Sheriff

Clerk

Defendant, a man accused of stealing a pig

Deputy King's Attorney

Farmer, owner of the missing hog and first witness for the prosecution

Seamstress, second witness for the prosecution

Tavern owner, a witness for the defense

12 jurors

4–12 justices

Courtroom audience

The Courthouse in Colonial Williamsburg, about 1771

Narrator (in hushed tones)**:** We are about to join the case of _____,
FULL NAME OF FARMER

hog owner, versus _____, accused hog thief.
FULL NAME OF DEFENDANT

Representing Mr. _____'s side in court is the Deputy King's Attorney.
LAST NAME OF FARMER

_____ must defend himself and call his own witnesses. He'll go
FULL NAME OF DEFENDANT

before this courtroom's Chief Justice, a panel of other justices—all of them merchants

and planters chosen to serve for life as our justices—and 12 men serving as today's

jurors. (whispering) And here come the judges now.

Chief Justice (entering room with other justices)**:** Sheriff _____, please call
LAST NAME OF SHERIFF

the court to order.

Sheriff: All rise! Oyez, oyez, oyez, silence is commanded in the court while His Majesty's

justices are sitting, upon pain of punishment. All manner of persons that have anything

to do at this court draw near and give your attendance, and if anyone have any plaint

to enter or suit to prosecute, let them come forth, and they shall be heard. God save

the King!

All: God save the King!

Clerk (standing and reading the criminal complaint)**:** To Your Honors, be it known on the

second of last month, _____ did knowingly and evilly steal a
FULL NAME OF DEFENDANT

hog belonging to _____. A complaint was made by the owner,
FULL NAME OF FARMER

and the sheriff, believing the complaint to be true, has arrested the defendant, and the

defendant is now ready to stand trial.

Name _____

Chief Justice: Bring the prisoner before the bar of His Majesty's justice.

(The sheriff brings in the defendant.)

Chief Justice *(to the defendant)***:** Do you understand the charges brought against you,

_____ ?
_{FULL NAME OF DEFENDANT}

Defendant: Yes.

Chief Justice: Make your plea.

Defendant: I am innocent, Your Honors.

Chief Justice: Do you want to be tried by commission of justices or upon the country?*

Defendant: Your Honors, I wish to be tried upon the country.

Chief Justice: Mr. King's Attorney, are you ready to make an opening statement?

Deputy King's Attorney: Your Honor, I shall prove the charge against the prisoner out of the mouths of two credible witnesses.

Chief Justice: Mr. _____, are you ready to make an opening statement?
_{LAST NAME OF DEFENDANT}

Defendant: Your Honors, I do not wish to make a statement.

Deputy King's Attorney: The Crown calls _____.
_{FULL NAME OF FARMER}

Sheriff: _____, come forth and be heard.
_{FULL NAME OF FARMER}

(The clerk hands the Bible to _____, who holds it in his right hand.)
_{FULL NAME OF FARMER}

Clerk: Do you, _____, swear the evidence you shall give is the truth,
_{FULL NAME OF FARMER}
the whole truth, and nothing but the truth, so help you God?

Farmer: I so swear. *(He returns the Bible to the clerk.)*

Deputy King's Attorney: Tell us what you know of the theft.

Farmer: Your Honors, I had trouble sleeping the night of the theft, so I was quite wide awake. The moon was full, the sky clear, and I could see very well even though it was night. I saw _____ steal one of my pigs, but I was too afraid of him to
_{FULL NAME OF DEFENDANT}
stop him. I clearly saw his face in the bright moonlight, and I likewise recognize the clothes he is wearing now as the same he wore that night.

Deputy King's Attorney: Thank you. No more questions.

Chief Justice: Mr. _____, do you have any questions?
_{LAST NAME OF DEFENDANT}

*If the defendant choses a commission of justices, there will be no jury, and a majority will prevail. A jury trial ("upon the country") requires a unanimous vote. The defendant stands a better chance of not being convicted if he or she selects a jury trial.

Colonial America Scholastic Professional Books

Defendant *(to farmer)*: Mr. _____, have you ever had a hog disappear, only to
FULL NAME OF FARMER
wander home on a later day?

Farmer: Many a time. But I saw you leading my pig away on a rope! This hog did not go missing of its own account.

Chief Justice *(to defendant)*: Do you have any more questions?

Defendant: No, Your Honors.

Chief Justice *(to farmer)*: You are dismissed.

Deputy King's Attorney: The Crown calls _____.
FULL NAME OF SEAMSTRESS

Sheriff: _____, come forth and be heard.
FULL NAME OF SEAMSTRESS

(The clerk hands the Bible to _____, who holds it in her right hand.)
FULL NAME OF SEAMSTRESS

Clerk: Do you, _____, swear the evidence you shall give is the truth,
FULL NAME OF SEAMSTRESS
the whole truth, and nothing but the truth, so help you God?

Seamstress: I so swear. *(She returns the Bible to the clerk.)*

Deputy King's Attorney: Tell us what you know of the theft.

Seamstress: I am a widow who makes a meager living sewing for others, sir. I was up late the
night of the evil deed, finishing a dress for the wife of a government leader, when I heard
the squeal of a hog. When I went to my window I saw that man *(she points to defendant)*
leading a pig on a rope.

(Courtroom audience murmurs.)

Deputy King's Attorney: Thank you. No more questions.

Chief Justice *(to defendant)*: Do you have any questions for the witness?

Defendant: No, Your Honors.

Chief Justice: _____, you are dismissed.
FULL NAME OF SEAMSTRESS

Deputy King's Attorney: Your Honors, having proven the Crown's case, the Crown rests.

Chief Justice: _____, do you have any witnesses?
FULL NAME OF DEFENDANT

Defendant: I call _____ to speak in my favor.
FULL NAME OF TAVERN OWNER

Sheriff: _____, come forth and be heard.
FULL NAME OF TAVERN OWNER

(The clerk hands the Bible to _____, who holds it in his right hand.)
FULL NAME OF TAVERN OWNER

Clerk: Do you, _____, swear the evidence you shall give is the truth, the
FULL NAME OF TAVERN OWNER
whole truth, and nothing but the truth, so help you God?

Tavern Owner: I so swear. *(Returns the Bible to the clerk.)*

Defendant: Are you not the owner and operator of the _____ Tavern here in
LAST NAME OF TAVERN OWNER
town, sir?

Tavern Owner: I am.

Defendant: Did I not partake of your tavern's good hospitality during the night of the second of last
month—*the night of the crime*?

Tavern Owner: You indeed did, my good sir. I remember well our conversation that evening.

(Crowd murmurs again.)

Deputy King's Attorney: Sir, is the defendant your kin?

Tavern Owner: By marriage only, sir. He wed my cousin last spring.

Chief Justice *(to the deputy king's attorney)*: Do you have any more questions?

Deputy King's Attorney: No, Your Honors.

Chief Justice: You, _____, are dismissed.
FULL NAME OF TAVERN OWNER

Chief Justice: Please summarize your cases, Mr. King's Attorney and Mr. _____
LAST NAME OF DEFENDANT
—and I remind you that we will entertain no new testimony.

Deputy King's Attorney: The defendant was clearly identified with the hog in question by both my
witnesses, each of whom is an upstanding citizen of our community, sir.

Defendant: My witness, _____, has said he saw and spoke with me during
FULL NAME OF TAVERN OWNER
the time of the crime. Therefore, I could not have committed it. Who would doubt the word of
_____, who with his tavern is one of the pillars of Williamsburg?
FULL NAME OF TAVERN OWNER

Chief Justice *(to the jury)*: Gentlemen of the jury, you and only you will make the decision whether or
not the defendant is innocent or guilty, and that is the only decision you will make. You will get
no food, no drink, no water, no light, and no heat until you return with an unanimous vote.

(The jury leaves the room.)

What is your verdict?
Is the defendant guilty or innocent?
Does the whole class agree with your conclusion?

Colonial America Scholastic Professional Books

Landowner

- Your family has lived in Virginia for five generations. You don't have any family in England anymore.
- You think Parliament has no right to tax the colonies.
- You think Virginians should be able to make their own laws for themselves.
- You're upset about the closing of the port of Boston.

Plantation Owner

- You think the British government does a lot for Virginia, and the taxes it charges colonists are necessary.
- Your wife is English, and all her family is in England.
- You don't want rebellion spreading from Massachusetts to Virginia and upsetting life.

Small Farmer

- You came from Germany. Loyalists and patriots both call you an "outsider," and you feel no ties to either side.
- You work hard every day just to feed your family. Who governs on top doesn't really affect your day-to-day life.
- You aren't very interested in whatever's going on in Boston between the patriots and British troops.

Merchant

- You sometimes sell goods that are imported from countries other than Britain—an act that is illegal under British law.
- Your customers are patriots. Some stores run by loyalists have been broken into.
- The Continental Association prohibiting the importation of British goods could shut down your store, but your neighbors are pressuring you to sign it.

Tailor

- You just arrived from Scotland, and all your family still lives there.
- Your customers are all loyalists. They all might leave if war breaks out. That would ruin your business.
- You're afraid of being punished for being a traitor to the King.

Middling Planter

- You're a Quaker. Your religion preaches against war or violence of any kind.
- You can't support fighting for or against the British and hope there will be a peaceful compromise.
- You own slaves. You wonder how the talk of freedom will affect slavery.

Daily Life

How a person lived in colonial America depended on a number of factors. When a person lived was one important factor. Early settlers had to work hard to establish homes and communities. They had few material goods compared to many people who lived at the time of the Revolution, when towns and cities were well established and many more consumer goods and services were available.

Where a person lived was another factor. Farm and frontier life was obviously more isolated than life in towns. Farm families sometimes made what little furniture and clothes they owned and raised much of what they ate—yet they still depended on merchants for things like tools and tea, sugar and shoes. They counted on gatherings at church for regular fellowship. Southern gentry families, who often lived along the rivers, could import items directly from England. Much of their time was spent supervising the slaves and servants who grew the crops and did most of the housework. In towns, "middling" people were more likely to work at trades and buy items at stores and markets, including food. Yet they also grew gardens and often raised cows, chickens, and pigs right in their backyards.

Life also varied from region to region. In New England colonies, for example, styles of dress, worship, schooling, and government were generally more egalitarian than in the southern colonies. Another big influence on how a person lived was his or her class and sex. Though advancing up the social ladder was easier in colonial America than Europe, women and men still had set roles to play within their classes.

Colonial Homes

Colonial homes were all-purpose spaces in which families, and their servants or slaves, lived, played, and worked. Many colonial houses were small, having only one to three rooms (plus the occasional small loft upstairs), with a fireplace that served for both heat and cooking. Toilet facilities, where there were any, could be outdoor "necessaries" (outhouses) or chamber pots that were used indoors and emptied outside the house. Some of these pots were hidden inside elegant furniture that looked like thrones.

Wood was the most plentiful and common house-building material in the southern colonies, but over time the northern colonists incorporated other materials like limestone or field rock into their house designs. By the mid-1600s, wealthy southern families had homes built of brick, and, in some places, separate buildings for servants' or slave quarters, smokehouses, washhouses, or kitchens. Log cabins were first built by Swedish colonists in Delaware and soon would become the home of choice for westward-bound pioneers.

A middle class family at home.

Many early colonists and poor or frontier families owned few possessions. Often, a home's only furnishings were a few stools or benches, a storage chest, and mattresses stuffed with cornhusks that were laid on the floor. (Sometimes an entire family—and whatever visitors were present—slept all crammed together on one mattress!) The family "dining table" was actually a board or boards, so that when mealtime came it was said that people sat "at the board" (as in the phrase "room and board"). Iron pots, dishes, cooking utensils, a few blankets, and a spare collection of tools hardly different from Roman times rounded out the average household's contents. (Forks weren't common until the 1700s and led one man to grumble that "God would not have given us fingers if He had wished us to use such an instrument.") The gentry possessed finer items in greater quantity and could afford to import furnishings from Europe or have them specially made by local tradesmen. Their homes might contain imported wallpaper, curtains, porcelain or pewter dishes, and feathered mattresses on canopied four-poster beds. Eighteenth-century urban dwellers of all classes tended to own more goods than did the rural "middling sort" and poor.

Colonial Clothes

The clothing people wore said a lot about them—what they did for a living, what social class they belonged to, and how wealthy they were. Wealthy people prided themselves on wearing clothing made of the finest European cloths and had their outfits tailored and retailored to copy the latest fashions overseas. Most colonists, however, wore simple clothes made of linen or wool. (The cotton gin wasn't invented until 1793, so cleaning cotton in order to spin it was very labor-intensive.) Making clothes was one of the responsibilities of women in some colonial households. Imported cloth was readily available, but when the colonists began to protest Britain's taxation policies before the Revolution, making and wearing homespun became a virture. Homespun was woven from flax (for linen) and fleece (for wool), then dyed with bark, roots, or berries to add color.

Before the mid-1700s, children wore clothes similar to those of their parents, modified for their age. By the 1760s, they were wearing special clothing that made it easier to play. Young children—both boys and girls—wore white dresses called "frocks." Toddlers sometimes wore padded caps called "pudding caps" to protect their heads if they fell. Boys started wearing pants when they were between the ages of three and seven. Girls continued to wear frocks. "Middling" and upper-class girls (and some boys), usually wore corsetlike garments called "stays" because people believed wearing stays helped promote good posture and supported the back.

Most men wore long linen shirts at night and during the day simply added a waistcoat (or vest), wool breeches that gathered at the knee, knitted stockings, and leather shoes or boots. A long coat was added for more formal occasions. Men wore straw hats to shade themselves from the sun if they worked in fields and caps if they were tradesmen. Wealthy men distinguished themselves by wearing hugely expensive wigs, velvet coats, shirts with lace ruffles, and silk stockings to show off their calves. Most women wore gowns (long dresses) or jackets (short gowns) made of linen or wool, with petticoats and a long linen shift underneath. They almost always kept their heads covered with a hat of some sort. Linen caps were the most common, but some wore straw or wool felt hats, often with their caps underneath. Women had long hair but usually kept it pinned up. By the time of the Revolution, wealthy women often had their hair piled high into elaborate hairstyles (forcing them, at times, to sleep in chairs in order to preserve their hairdos) and wore stays, low-necked dresses trimmed in lace, and silk shoes.

Household slaves were sometimes given hand-me-downs from their masters, or cloth from which they were to make their own clothing. Some male household slaves in gentry families wore livery. Field slaves had to make do with flimsy shifts and breeches that provided little warmth on cold winter days. Yet some slaves crafted their own sense of style by creating boldly colored outfits from assorted scraps and ribbons, which they wore on special occasions. Women and girls also braided their hair into beautiful styles based on African patterns. Both men and women, though, often kept their heads covered with cloth or hats while working.

Colonial Food

Though the colonists came from Europe, their diet was soon "Americanized." Corn, a New World food adopted from the Indians, quickly became a staple. Whole corn was ground into meal, and cornmeal turned into breakfast "mush" and cornbread. Poor families, servants, and slaves ate some meat but mostly corn, beans, and vegetables they grew in gardens. Cooking was done by women over open fireplaces where large pots were hung. Breakfast was usually mush or johnny cakes (cornmeal pancakes) and perhaps a bit of ham or bacon. The main meal of the day took place in the early afternoon. It was often a stew of meat and vegetables cooked in a large pot, though wealthy colonists would lay a more elaborate table of roasted meats and vegetables. For supper, families ate leftovers and bread. Colonists had few methods of preserving foods, so what was eaten depended mostly on what was seasonally available. However, some meats were salted and dried or smoked, and carrots, squash, turnips, apples, and pears were kept in cool, dry root cellars dug into the ground or below the house.

Kitchens in colonial America featured large fireplaces for cooking and heat.

Schooling

Most colonial children learned the basic life skills they would need as adults from their parents or other relatives. Mothers of all classes taught their daughters how to cook, sew, garden, spin, and care for chickens and cows. Boys learned how to hunt, farm, and make tools and equipment from their fathers. A tradesman would teach his sons his trade, or a son might be sent to apprentice with some other master. Children of the gentry usually went to school or were taught by a private tutor. They were expected to know how to read, write, and "cipher" (basic arithmetic). In Virginia dancing masters taught them the stately minuet, the latest country dances, and deportment. Music masters taught them to play a genteel instrument. Some learned one of the languages of western Europe. "Well-bred" boys were expected to learn Latin and attend college at colonial institutions like the College of William and Mary in Williamsburg and Harvard in Massachusetts or at universities in England.

By contrast, formal education at its most basic level remained a luxury for poorer people throughout much of the colonial period. Schools weren't cheap to run or attend. Besides, many children were needed at home to help keep their household or farm running. If parents knew how to read and write, they often taught their children at home—though many families owned no books except the Bible and maybe an almanac. Yet given these spartan conditions, many colonial boys and girls learned at least some of the basic skills of reading, writing, and arithmetic.

Religion

Religious practices varied widely within the colonies. Colonies like Virginia were under mandate from the king that the Church of England (the Anglican church) be their official church. By law all heads of households were to attend service at least once a month or be fined. (Although, in eighteenth-century Virginia religious groups such as the Baptists and Presbyterians exerted increasing influence.) The Puritans, who left Europe so they could worship as they saw fit, estab-

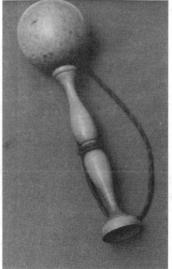

Left: Children playing a game of Goose
Right: Bilbo catchers were popular toys for children in colonial America.

lished the Congregational church as the official church in Connecticut, Massachusetts, and New Hampshire. Other colonies, such as Pennsylvania (founded by Quakers) and Maryland (founded by Catholics), were relatively more accepting of different Christian groups and traditions. This was almost a necessity as waves of non-English immigrants with their own traditions began settling in the colonies. But no matter whether a colonist was Catholic, Puritan, Anglican, or Moravian, free or a slave, Sunday was a day for worship, fellowship, and rest. Church seating was often assigned by social class or segregated by sex or race. Socializing before and after services was an important way for people to exchange news and meet neighbors, and for young people to court.

Travel and Communication

Colonists traveled little by today's standards, yet each trip took much more effort than we can imagine. Up through the 1600s, roads were few and far between. Most were dirt tracks that once had been Indian trails, and there were few bridges. Ferries provided transportation across rivers. By the mid-1700s, however, there were stagecoach lines or boat routes running between many colonial cities, especially in the more densely populated Northeast.

Early colonists passed news and letters along as best they could. Notices were posted on public building doors, and announcements were made at church. Travelers were asked to carry letters to inns or taverns in the next town, where they left them to be claimed. The British government permitted a postal system to be set up in 1691, though service to rural, and especially southern, areas developed slowly. Ben Franklin became deputy postmaster general for the colonies in 1753 and was said to greatly improve the postal service's speed and frequency. Newspapers became a common form of spreading information in the 1700s, as well.

Leisure

Life for colonists was filled with hard work. Yet life had its pleasures, too. At barn raisings and corn-huskings, families would work hard communally but then enjoy feasting and dancing, games and gossip together. Weddings and christenings were joyful occasions. Dancing in the formal European style was also very popular among the gentry, who considered graceful dancers to be especially refined and cultured. Men also enjoyed meeting at taverns to drink, talk politics, read newspapers, and play billiards and cards. (Few women participated in the boys' club environment of taverns.) Horse racing was also a hugely popular spectator sport. Although children had few toys by today's standards, they found many ways to entertain themselves. Marble games were popular, as were ball games, kite flying, hoop rolling, and playing with dolls, whether made of corncobs or imported porcelain.

A FEW COLONIAL HOLIDAYS

Lady Day, March 25—This day celebrated the announcement made to the Virgin Mary that she would give birth to Jesus. It was also the day when tenant farmers struck up new arrangements with their landowners.

Midsummer, June 24—Some towns celebrated this day by lighting bonfires. Some believed that ghosts and fairies came out on this night. On the night before, girls were supposed to be able to discover if their boyfriends really loved them by hanging a plant called orpine in their house.

Michaelmas, September 29—British families celebrated this day, also known as the feast day of St. Michael the Archangel, by feasting on a goose.

Holiday celebrations varied throughout the colonies. British settlers celebrated the traditional English holidays mentioned in the box above. They also observed Good Friday, Easter, St. Valentine's Day, and other holidays. Christmas, though, was celebrated differently from place to place. The Puritans passed laws against celebrating Christmas, as they believed only Sunday was a special day. Settlers in the middle and southern colonies, by contrast, welcomed Christmas with feasting, worshiping, some gift giving (often in the days after Christmas), and some weddings as well. No one yet celebrated Christmas with a tree, as that custom would be introduced in the mid-1800s.

Student Activities

Fashions of the Times

You could tell a great deal about people during colonial times by the clothes they wore. Most ordinary people owned very few clothes because they were expensive and/or time-consuming to make. Wealthy people, meanwhile, spent large sums on well-tailored outfits made of velvet, silk, satin, handmade lace, and other imported goods. In this activity, students review types of colonial clothing as well as make the connection between colonial fashions and status in society.

Materials
Fashions of the Times (pages 48–49), scissors

Here's How

1. Begin by discussing with students what fashions today make people stand out as especially "hip." What kinds of clothing indicate that a person has lots of money? Are "cool" fashions and "rich" fashions always one and the same these days? Explain that in colonial times, you could always tell who was wealthy or privileged—and who was not—by looking at their clothes.

2. Distribute a copy of Fashions of the Times to students and have them complete the activities.

3. Ask students how the use of expensive fabrics would have changed the look of these basic fashions. Last, discuss similarities and differences between colonial clothing and fashions today.

Caps and Cravats

Colonial women usually covered their heads, whether they were inside or outside. Ordinary women often made do with a simple linen or cotton cap. Men of all classes, meanwhile, often wore a scarf around their neck called a cravat or a neckband called stock. Simple versions were little more than strips of white muslin, while more expensive varieties came in linen edged with lace or embroidery. In this activity, students put their math and measuring skills to work making caps, then exercise spatial reasoning and, later, the skill of writing clear directions as they learn to tie their own colonial-style cravats.

Materials for Caps

Oak tag or butcher paper cut into 20-inch squares, pencils, rulers, compasses (optional), scissors, hole punch, white muslin cloth cut into 20-inch squares, ribbon or yarn cut into 4-foot lengths

Here's How for Caps

1. Give each student a square of oak tag or butcher paper. Fold the square into quarters to find its center point. Mark it with a dot.

2. Measure out 9 inches from the center dot along a fold and mark this spot (the radius). Pivot the ruler 2 to 3 inches around the center dot, marking the 9-inch radius, until the marks make a complete circle.

3. Connect the dots to make a circle (or use a compass) and cut it out.

4. Measure out 7 inches from the center of the cut-out circle and mark this spot with a dot. Repeat this every 1½ inches until the marks make a complete circle of dots.

5. Punch holes for each dot in the circle. See finished pattern below.

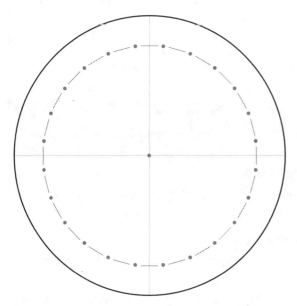

6. Hand out the cloth squares. Trace the pattern's outer circumference on the cloth and mark each punch hole.

7. Cut out the circle and punch holes or cut slits at each hole punch site.

8. Thread ribbon or yarn in and out through the holes, bunching the material into a cap as you go.

9. Fit the cap on each student's head and adjust the yarn or ribbon, tying it in front.

Materials for Cravats

White muslin cloth (or old, clean sheets, preferably white) cut into strips 4 or 5 inches wide by 5 feet long, Ties That Bind (page 50), large mirror, if possible

Here's How for Cravats

1. Give each student a strip of fabric, plus a copy of Ties that Bind.

2. Divide students into small groups so they can help one another follow the directions. Encourage them to try different tying configurations and then draw instructions that show how they achieved their new looks.

NOTE: Before students begin tying, warn them not to play with other students' cravats, as the neck is obviously a sensitive part of the body.

FABRICS OF THEIR LIVES

Rich and poor colonists wore similar clothing styles in everyday life—men in their breeches, waistcoats, and cravats or stocks, women in their shifts, petticoats, and gowns. The big difference lay in the quality of tailoring and the type of fabrics used in the outfits (not to mention the number of outfits owned by one person). While ordinary people's clothes were usually rough-spun wool or linen, wealthy colonists could afford to wear outfits made of imported silk, satin, velvet, and handmade lace. Their buttons were silver, pewter, or brass, and expensive gold or silver trim often edged their clothes.

🏠 Build a Battledore

Children fortunate enough to attend school during colonial times wouldn't find many materials there. Young students often learned their letters and numbers from a hornbook or battledore—sturdy hand-held paddles or booklets that featured the alphabet, numbers, a poem, a Bible verse, and perhaps some pictures. In this activity, students make their own colonial battledores.

Materials

Build a Battledore (page 51), poster board or heavy construction paper, scissors, glue or paste, colored markers

Here's How

1. Have students make a list on the board of all the books, reference books, and computer tools they use at school every day. Then point out that during colonial times students often brought their own books, and that many families owned just a few books. The only individual study aid many beginning students had was a hornbook or battledore. Show a sample battledore that you have already constructed.

2. Distribute a copy of Build a Battledore to each student, along with art supplies. On the front of the battledore, have students add simple pictures and sentences. (See example above.)

3. Ask students to describe all the things they can think of that colonial students could have learned from battledores. *(capital letters, lowercase letters, vowels, numbers, sounds)* What does the teaching style of battledores share in common with educational TV shows like *Sesame Street*? How is it different? Help students under-

stand that while battledores were simple and spare, given their size, they were well thought out.

EXTENSION ACTIVITY

Challenge students to design a modern-day battledore of their own, updating the images used to represent letters and giving it an eye-catching cover.

🏠 Goosey Game

In colonial times the "Game of the Goose" was a very popular board game in Europe and the colonies. In the adult version, money was won and lost as players raced around the board toward the center finish point. In this adaptation of the game, the first player to reach the end wins. (Adapted from *A Colonial Williamsburg Activities Book* by Pat Fortunato, Colonial Williamsburg Foundation, 1982.)

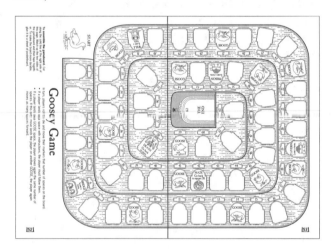

Materials

Goosey Game (pages 52–53), dice (1 die per group), markers (seeds, buttons, coins)

Here's How

1. Divide students into groups of 3 or 4 players and provide each group with a copy of Goosey Game, a die, and markers. Have students follow the directions on the reproducible to assemble their game boards.

2. Have each student roll the die. The player who scores highest goes first, and the turns proceed around to the player's left.

3. The first player rolls the die and moves his or her marker as many spaces on the board. If a player lands on a space with instructions, he or she must follow them. If a player lands on a GOOSE space, he or she moves again the same number of spaces. If the player lands on another GOOSE, he or she again moves as many spaces forward.

Reading the News

Newspapers during colonial times published news from Europe and the other colonies as well as local announcements and advertisements. In this activity, students gain insight into colonial society by reading actual advertisements from the March 3, 1774, issue of the *Virginia Gazette*, published in Williamsburg. The issue's editor and publisher was Clementina Rind, the printer highlighted in the People of Williamsburg profile cards introduced earlier (page 19).

Materials
Reading the News (page 54), issues of the local newspaper

Here's How
1. Divide the class into small groups. Ask the class why people read newspapers today. *(for news, sports info, gossip, comics, ads)* How much of a newspaper these days is actually made up of advertisements? Have students estimate an answer. Then distribute an issue of the local newspaper to each group and have them come up with a rough estimate of the ratio of news to ads (including not just classifieds but big corporate ads). Help students conclude that newspapers devote approximately half their space to ads—not an entirely bad thing, since the ads let readers know what is available and/or going on in their community.

2. Now shift the discussion to colonial newspapers. Do students think that newspapers then were less or more important than they are now? Draw students' attention to the fact that during colonial times, there were few ways for news and announcements to be broadcast. There was no TV or radio, let alone CNN or the Internet.

People depended on newspapers for information and news. As people talked about what was in the newspapers, the information quickly found its way into the community. Not everyone could afford newspapers or even read, so word of mouth was still an important way of spreading the news.

3. Distribute a copy of Reading the News to each student. Have them read the ads and complete the questions.

4. Review the ads and the questions as a class, checking for understanding. Have volunteers sum up what the descriptions of slaves in the ads reveal about colonial attitudes toward enslaved peoples and slavery.

Answers to Reading the News: 1. B **2.** cash **3.** D **4.** A person has died. **5.** Answers will vary.

Colonial Cup-and-Ball Toy

Colonial children played with many different kinds of toys. Dolls were made from rags or cornhusks with wood-carved heads. Balls, tops, marbles, toy soldiers, tea sets, and tin whistles were all sold by colonial merchants. One popular toy was called a bilbo catcher, from the French word *bilboquet* for a similar toy. It was a string with a ball tied to one end and a cup attached to the other end. The object was to toss the ball into the air and catch it in the cup. Students make and play with their own bilbo catchers in this activity. (Adapted from *A Colonial Williamsburg Activities Book* by Jean Bethell and Susan Axtell, Colonial Williamsburg Foundation, 1984.)

Materials
Sharpened pencil; paper cups; 12-inch lengths of string; tape; metal washers, nuts, or buttons

Here's How
1. Use a sharpened pencil to poke a hole in the center of a paper cup's bottom. Thread the string through and knot it inside the cup. Put a piece of tape over the knot to secure it.

2. Tie the metal washer, nut, or button to the other end of the string. The bilbo catcher is finished.

3. To play, simply hold the paper cup in one hand, swing the washer out away from you, and try to catch it in the cup. Practice makes perfect!

4. Invite students to decorate their cups by drawing colonial scenes or patterns on a strip of paper and then using it to cover the cup.

EXTENSION ACTIVITY

Invite students to play with other colonial toys, such as tops and marbles. (See marble game on page 13.)

Dancing "The First of April"

Dancing was an important part of colonial social life. Balls and dance parties provided opportunities for people to meet and young people to court in a supervised atmosphere. Among the gentry, dancing skills were a mark of good breeding and refinement, and rare was the person in many colonies who didn't dance. Virginia colonists were especially renowned for their love of dancing. "The First of April" was a popular dance in Williamsburg during the late 1700s. Students learn and practice an adaptation of the dance in this activity. Consider involving a music teacher to make this activity even more successful. (Adapted from the Colonial Williamsburg Foundation's Teaching Unit *Six Colonial Dances*.)

Dancing Facts

- All colonial dances started out with "courtesies"—men bowed and women curtsied. A man bowed by extending one leg forward and bending forward at the waist, arms extended from the body. (The back leg should bend while the extended leg remains straight.) A woman curtsied by placing her heels together with the toes pointed out to form a V, holding her skirt with her hands, then bending her knees with her back straight, chin up, and eyes lowered in modesty.

- Eye contact was very important during dancing. Dancers always made eye contact with their partners during the dance.

- When "holding hands," the men held their hands palms up and the women palms down.

Here's How

1. Begin this activity by having students describe or—better yet—briefly demonstrate dance styles or moves that are currently in vogue. Explain that dancing was also very popular in colonial times, though the moves were very, very different.

2. Divide the class into groups of four students—two boy-girl couples. (If this is a problem—and it can be, depending on students' level of maturity—make groups all-boys or all-girls and assign the partners A-B designations.) Consider working with only two or three groups at a time at first to ease the class into learning.

3. Instruct all the boys to line up on the left and the girls across from them on the right.

4. **Courtesies:** Help boys bow and girls curtsy.

5. **Four Hands Across:** Within each group, each dancer reaches diagonally across with the *right* hand to take his or her *non*-partner's hand. (See "Dancing Facts" for details on the etiquette of taking hands.) They then circle clockwise, ending up where they started.

6. **Left Hands Back:** Within each group, each dancer reaches diagonally across with the *left* hand to take his or her *non*-partner's hand. They circle counterclockwise, ending up where they started.

7. **Down the Center and Back:** The head couple joins both hands, faces toward the set-center, and walks down between the other dancers to the center of the set. Once there, they drop hands, turn and face each other, retake hands, face toward the top, walk back up to where they started, and drop hands.

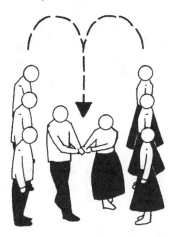

8. **Cast Down:** The head couple turns away from each other and toward the top of the set. They proceed to the outside of the line and walk behind the other dancers toward the bottom of the set.

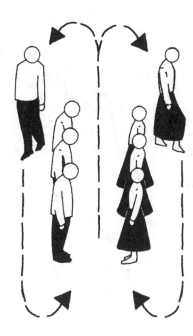

9. Repeat steps 5–8 until all the couples have been the head couple.

EXTENSION ACTIVITY

Once students have mastered the basic style of "The First of April," challenge them to carry it out to the beat of their favorite songs. Why is it next to impossible with some songs? What does that say about how rhythms in music have changed since colonial times?

A Colonial Celebration

Plan a class colonial celebration for students and their families. The party will allow students to integrate the various themes of colonial life they have been studying. They can dance "The First of April," perhaps wearing their caps and cravats, and attempt to teach family members a few of the dance moves as well. For food, prepare the dessert below, and perhaps provide samples of other foods from the time (for example, cornbread, apple butter, snickerdoodle cookies).

Colonial Cookies

Making and eating colonial foods is a great way to "get a taste" for colonial life. Below is a recipe for gingerbread cookies to make with your class, or have them make at home with their families. Gingerbread cookies were a treat served at parties and special occasions. Presentation was an important part of setting a table in fine colonial homes. Cookies were sometimes stacked into a pyramid on a table an edible decoration.

Materials
Colonial Cookies (page 55)

Here's How

1. Distribute a copy of Colonial Cookies to each student. If an in-class cooking session isn't feasible, send the recipe home with students to make the cookies with the help of an adult. Encourage those who do to bring in samples for the class to try.

2. Have students who completed the cooking assignment share their experiences making the recipe and how they liked the cookies. •

Fashions of the Times

Can you figure out how to get these colonists dressed? Read the captions to become familiar with clothing basics they wore every day. Figure out the order the clothes must have been worn in. Then cut out the pieces and try to put them correctly on each figure.

petticoat

cap

hat

pockets

gown

shift

apron

Colonial America   Scholastic Professional Books

Fashions of the Times

Can you figure out how to get these colonists dressed? Read the captions to become familiar with clothing basics they wore every day. Figure out the order the clothes must have been worn in. Then cut out the pieces and try to put them correctly on each figure.

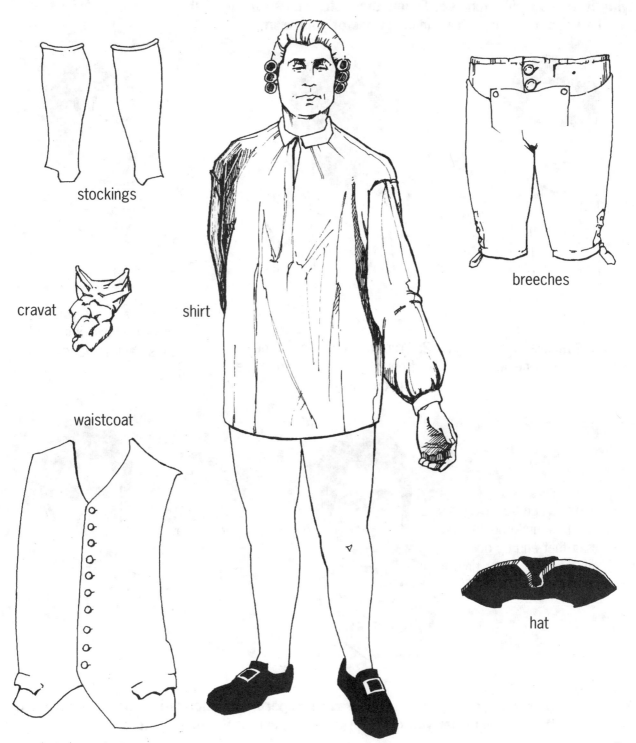

stockings

cravat

shirt

breeches

waistcoat

hat

Ties That Bind

Men of all ranks in colonial society wore scarves around their necks. One kind of scarf was called a cravat (kruh-VAHT). There was an art to tying it, as you will soon see. Follow the instructions for the first style. Then see if you can draw instructions of your own.

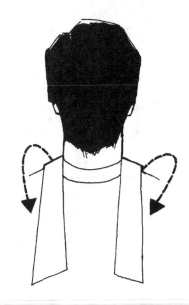

3. Tie the ends as you begin to tie your shoelaces and bring ends back to your chest.

1. Hang the middle of the cravat around your neck.

2. Wrap the ends around the front of your neck and drape on your back.

4. Cross left end over right end, tuck underneath, and bring that end up behind and over the upper ring of cloth around your neck.

5. Straighten your cravat.

How else could you tie your cravat? Experiment, then write and draw instructions that explain what you did. Work with a partner if you want to want to.

Colonial America   Scholastic Professional Books

Colonial America   Scholastic Professional Books

Build a Battledore

A battledore was a booklet colonial students used to learn how to read. Often, it was the only "book" they owned. What kinds of reading skills did it teach them?

To make a battledore:
1. Glue this page securely to poster board or heavy paper.
2. Cut out the battledore.
3. Fold along the dotted lines.
3. On the front of your battledore, add a few simple sentences and pictures to illustrate them.

Ape	Bear	Cow	Dog
Elke	Fox	Goat	Hare
Ibex	Jay	Kite	Lion
Magpye	Nag	Ounce	Plover
Quail	Ruff	Snipe	Teal
Unicorn	Weefil	Yellow-hammer	Zebra

a b c d e f g h i j k l m n
o p q r s t u v w x y z

A B C D E F G H I J K L M N
O P Q R S T U V W X Y Z

*A B C D E F G H I J K L M N
O P Q R S T U V W X Y Z*

*a b c d e f g h i j k l m n
o p q r s t u v v x y z*

a e i o u y
ab eb ib ob ub   ba be bi bo bu
ac ec ic oc uc   ca ce ci co cu
ad ed id od ud   da de di do du

1 2 3 4 5 6 7 8 9 0

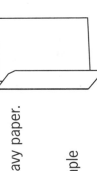
Ape

Bear

Cock

Dog

51

Goosey Game

In turn, players roll the die and move their markers that number of spaces on the board.

- If a player lands on a space with instructions, the player must follow them.
- If a player lands on a GOOSE space, the player moves again the same number of spaces. If this extra move lands the player on another GOOSE, the player again moves the same number of spaces forward.

To assemble the game board: Cut along the solid line at the right side of this page. Match the two sides of the game board and then tape together. To make the board more durable, glue it to a sheet of poster board.

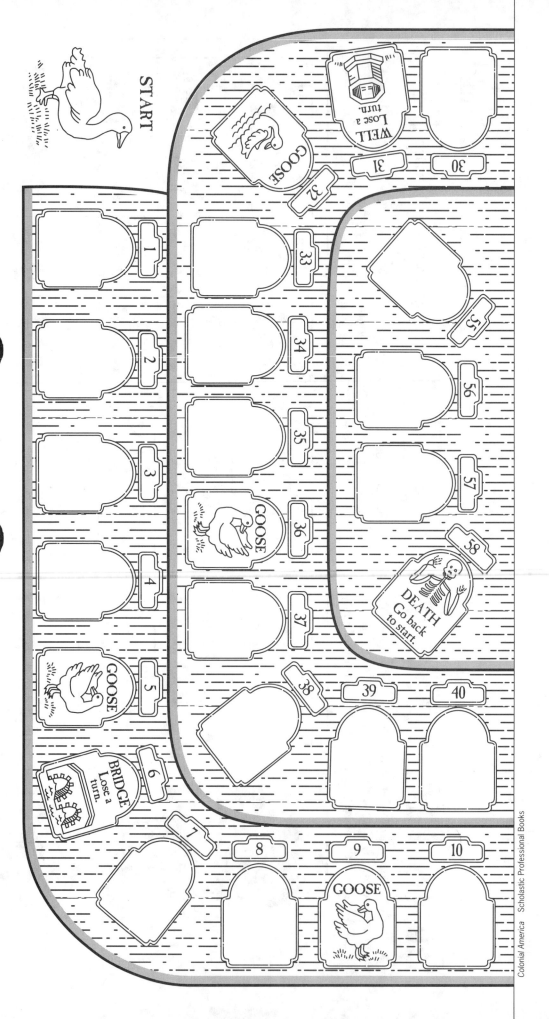

START

Colonial America   Scholastic Professional Books

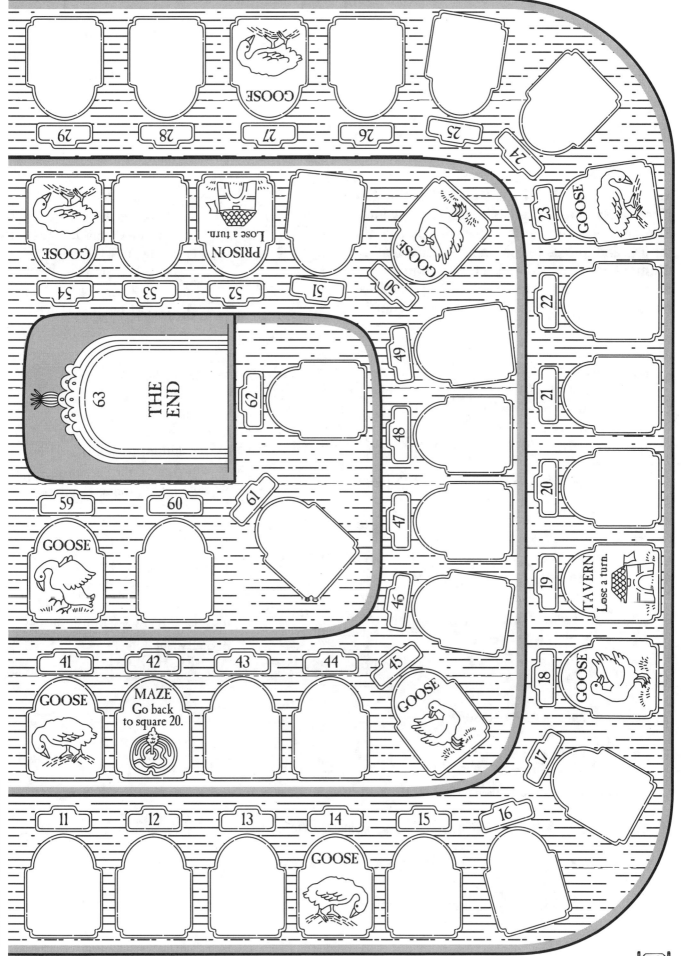

29 28 27 GOOSE 26 25 24

54 GOOSE 53 52 PRISON Lose a turn. 51 50 GOOSE 23 GOOSE 22 21 20 19 TAVERN Lose a turn. 18 GOOSE 17

63 THE END 62 49 48 47 46

59 60 61

GOOSE

41 GOOSE 42 MAZE Go back to square 20. 43 44 45 GOOSE

11 12 13 14 GOOSE 15 16

Reading the News

Colonists counted on newspapers for world and local news. In a 1774 issue of Williamsburg's *Virginia Gazette*, colonists read about events in Europe, the arrival of the governor of Virginia's family, and letters to the paper's editor, Mrs. Clementina Rind. They also could read an entire page of advertisements, such as the ones on this page. Why were ads important?

A
EDWARD WALL—An eminent tailor (lives in Richmond county, near Farnham church), begs leave to inform the public that he has just imported all the newest fashions from London... READY MONEY, OR SHORT CREDIT. Those ladies and gentlemen who please to favour him with their business may depend on having their work done in the neatest and best manner.

B
Strayed some time ago, a small dark mare, one of her hind feet white, 4 feet 6 or 7 inches height, with a small star in her forehead, is 4 years old, not branded. Whoever brings the said mare to me, living near Col. Harwood's mill, in Warwick county, shall have twenty shillings. WILLIAM CLARK

C
To be sold, at public sale on Wednesday the 30th of March, at Eagle's Nest in Stafford, fashionable plates and all the household and kitchen furniture. Also, several valuable slaves, men, women, and children. Credit will be given till the 30th of March 1776... Contact the Honorable John Taylor, the executor of Charles Carter, deceased, and Joseph Jones, Esquire.

D
A sober, well-disposed man, capable of teaching children to read and write, may meet with employment by application to Charles Carter, of Corotoman, Lancaster county.

E
Run away... in April last, a Virginia-born Negro named Charles, of small stature, about 50 years of age, a little grey... by trade a shoemaker. He... had a wife at Colonel Gawin Corbin's, which makes it probable he is lurking in that neighborhood... Whoever will convey him to me, at Morattico, in Lancaster county, shall have a reward of FIVE POUNDS ... RAWLEIGH DOWNMAN.

1. Which ad regards a lost horse? _____

2. What do you think "ready money" means in ad A? _____

3. Which ad is like a modern-day want ad for a job? _____

4. Why are slaves and all belongings in a house being sold in ad C? _____

5. What does the size of the reward offered for the capture of Charles say about the value of enslaved

   people to their masters? _____

   _____

Colonial America   Scholastic Professional Books

Colonial Cookies

Gingerbread cookies were a special treat at colonial parties. Hostesses often stacked up the cookies in the shape of a pyramid to make a soon-to-be-eaten decoration. Try this recipe with an adult.

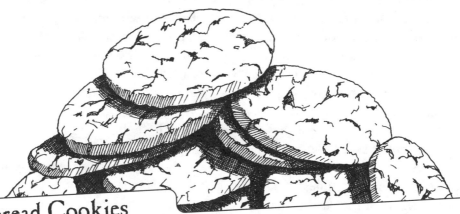

Gingerbread Cookies

Ingredients
1 c. sugar
2 tsp. ginger
1 tsp. nutmeg
1 tsp. cinnamon
½ tsp. salt
1½ tsp. baking soda
½ c. evaporated milk
1 c. melted butter
1 c. molasses
1 tsp. vanilla
4 c. flour

To Make
1. Combine the sugar, spices, salt, and baking soda in a large mixing bowl.
2. Add in the evaporated milk, melted butter, molasses, and vanilla. Mix well.
3. Stir in the flour one cup at a time, mixing well. Add extra flour if the mixture is still sticky after adding the 4 cups.
4. Knead the dough for a minute or two.
5. Roll out the dough to ¼-inch thickness and cut into cookies. They can be any shape, though circles stack well.
6. Bake on greased cookie sheets at 375°F for 10–12 minutes.
7. Let the cookies cool and stack into a pyramid before eating.

Colonial America   Scholastic Professional Books

Digging Into the Past

How do we know what we know about colonial America? Historians and archaeologists collect information about the past in many ways. One way is by studying surviving documents from colonial times. Letters written between family members and diaries let historians learn about daily activities as well as what people thought of politics and religion at the time. Preserved store receipts and ledgers give us an idea of what people purchased every day and what were extravagant luxuries. Newspapers and official documents tell of deaths, births, crimes, and laws in the colonies. Some of these documents have been kept in special libraries or museums. Others have been found in old houses or have been passed down through families.

Archaeologists learn about the past through things that people have left behind. Artifacts, building foundations, and old wells are all examples of physical evidence that carries information about how people once lived. Over time, artifacts and features like these become buried under layers of soil. About 8 to 12 inches of soil piles up every 100 years, so most colonial artifacts are only about two feet below the surface. Many are found when construction crews dig down to lay pipe or build basements. Farmers sometimes find a piece of pottery or a nail while plowing a field. Finding an artifact and documents such as old maps and floor plans can tell archaeologists where they should dig an excavation site. Archaeologists often find many broken plates, bottles, nails, animal bones, and other artifacts when they uncover old trash pits behind colonial homes. Animal bones can tell us what kind of meats people were eating, and pottery can help to date a site. Each artifact is full of information.

Archaeological excavations are slow, painstaking work. Layers of soil must be carefully removed, and excavators must note the exact location and depth of anything found. After all, a site can be dug only once! All the artifacts are taken to a laboratory, where they are preserved or restored and then studied. Broken pots are reassembled, bones are identified, and objects are dated. In this way, archaeologists attempt to reconstruct the past from what was left behind.

Archaeologists dig for artifacts at a site in Colonial Williamsburg.

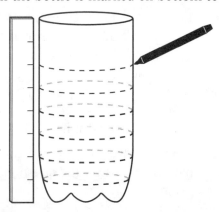

Above: A wine bottle uncovered at an archaeological site.
Left: Workers make a discovery at the site.

Student Activities

Time in a Bottle

Understanding that "deeper is older" is an important part of archaeology. Student archaeologists get firsthand experience excavating and inferring relative age in this activity.

Materials

2-liter plastic bottles with the tops cut off, soils (sand, potting soil, and so on), "artifacts" (coins, buttons, pottery shards, bottle caps), newspaper, ruler, permanent markers, Time in a Bottle (page 60), spoons, craft sticks, paintbrushes, plastic grocery bags

Here's How

1. Divide students into groups of two or three. Each will need a bottle, soils, and six different artifacts. (Protect the tables with newspaper.)

2. Stand a ruler next to the bottle and mark the bottle at 1 inch from the bottom. Do this all the way around the bottle so there's a ring at 1 inch. Repeat for 2 inches, 3 inches, 4 inches, and so on until the bottle is marked off bottom to top.

3. Explain to students that they are going to make future excavation sites. Have them layer the bottle with soils and artifacts. Make sure they pack down the soil well with their fists as they go.

THE FRENCHMAN'S MAP

In 1909, an old map was donated to the College of William and Mary in Williamsburg. It was a map of the town drawn in 1781 by a French soldier who was assigning winter quarters for troops during the Revolutionary War. It shows Williamsburg's three main streets and cross streets and the buildings along them. There are also creeks, ravines, and yards marked. This map was a great help in the restoration of Colonial Williamsburg. Archaeologists used the map to decide where to dig for original foundations and where to reconstruct buildings.

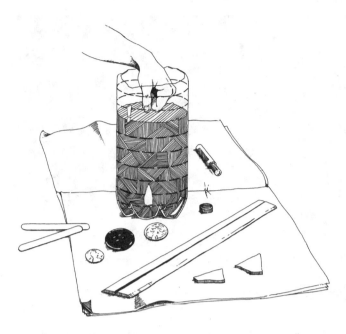

4. Collect and redistribute the bottles so no group has their own. Distribute a copy of Time in a Bottle to each group, along with spoons, craft sticks, paintbrushes, and plastic grocery bags.

5. Explain to students that they are going to carefully remove all the soil layer by layer with a spoon (disposing of it in their grocery sack), uncovering artifacts as they go. When they find something, they need to stop and draw it on Time in a Bottle exactly where in the bottle they found it and noting the depth. Ready, excavate!

6. Once the groups have completely excavated their bottles, have them answer the questions. Check for understanding.

Artifact Facts

Finding an artifact is just the beginning of uncovering its secrets. Archaeologists must then try to determine what the object might have been used for and what that tells us about the people who left it. For example, uncovering a letter seal conveys that whoever owned it could read and write, that this person could obtain wax to use it, and that he or she sent letters that demanded privacy. A coat of arms on the seal would identify the family as gentry and allow the archaeologist to identify the family name. In this activity, students infer what

actual colonial artifacts might have been used for. (Adapted from The Colonial Williamsburg Foundation's Teaching Unit, *Clues from the Past*.)

Materials
What Could It Be? (page 61)

Here's How

1. Divide the class into groups of three. Distribute a copy of What Could It Be? to each group.

2. Ask students to carefully study the two artifacts at the top of the page. Inform them that the artifacts are life-sized and that the material each is made of is written in the chart.

3. Challenge groups to fill in the chart. Encourage them to make "educated guesses." It's okay not to know.

4. When students have completed the chart to the best of their ability, tell them the following. Artifact 1 is a wig curler. Wig hair was set on clay curlers like these to give it curl. Sometimes the wigs with curlers were wrapped in cloth, covered in bread dough, and baked to set the curls! Artifact 2 is a jaw harp. It's a musical instrument that has been around since the Middle Ages. It's held in the mouth and played.

EXTENSION ACTIVITY

Design a similar chart to allow students to deduce the function of modern appliances. Kitchen gadgets, sewing notions, office supplies, and specialty tools work well.

Puzzling Evidence

When archaeologists find artifacts, they are often broken into many pieces. All the pieces are carefully collected, labeled, and later put together like a puzzle. But because often not all the pieces are there, archaeologists have to "fill in the blanks." Students cut out and assemble pieces of an eighteenth-century dinner plate and draw in the missing parts in this activity. (Adapted from *Archaeology for Young Explorers* by Patricia Samford and David L. Ribblett, The Colonial Williamsburg Foundation, 1995.)

Materials

Puzzling Evidence (page 62); sheets of white paper, pencils, glue, scissors, crayons, markers, colored pencils

Here's How

1. Reproduce and distribute Puzzling Evidence to students, along with blank sheets of paper, glue, and scissors.

2. Have students cut out the puzzle pieces.

3. Place the pieces on the paper and fit them together. Paste them to the paper.

4. Challenge students to finish the plate by drawing in what they believe is missing. Suggest that they use the rest of the plate as a guide. Ask: *What kind of plate does this seem to have been—cheap, expensive? Why do you think so? What do you think people might have used it for? Why? What kind of family might it have belonged to?*

5. Explain that wealthy colonial families liked to display and use ceramic dishes made in England or Holland. Often, these dishes were colored blue and white and decorated to resemble the more expensive porcelain made in China. Ordinary dishes, by contrast, were usually made of coarser clays and decorated with less costly glazes. Although Colonial Williamsburg archaeologists have found a variety of pottery shards in old trash pits, the majority of these pieces are of the less costly pottery. That's because servants and family were much more careful with their expensive dinnerware.

6. Invite students to color their plates.

Hunting for History

Finding out about a historical building, place, person, or event often starts at the library. Invite students to investigate a colonial person, place, or thing in this activity. Topics of investigation might include a person like George Washington; a place like Williamsburg, Virginia; a trade like blacksmithing, bookbinding, or weaving; a type of architecture, like log cabins; technology, like the development of frontier rifles; colonial fashions; or foods, games, or chores—the possibilities are endless.

Materials

Hunting for History (page 63), access to library, encyclopedias, books, reference tools

Here's How

1. Ask students how they might find out about something from the past. List all the possible resources that might be used: books, encyclopedias, magazines, museums, CD-ROMS, the Internet, and so on.

2. Distribute a copy of Hunting for History to each student. Assign, or assist students in choosing, a person, place, or event to research. (The timeline on pages 6–9 suggests a number of topic ideas.)

3. Challenge students to fill out their sheets at the library or using classroom books.

4. Invite students to present their information to the class. If multiple students have the same topics, they can pool their information and present together.

5. Challenge students to produce a short report about their topic using the research tools they have discovered.

EXTENSION ACTIVITY

If possible, have students compile their research into a "Resources on Colonial America" Web page to post on the Internet. (If going on-line isn't feasible, they could make an information booklet, which your school librarian might agree to display.) Students will need to work together to organize their information into useful categories and write clear instructions explaining what their Internet site or booklet is and how it can be used.

Name _____

Time in a Bottle

Carefully remove soil from your bottle with a spoon, putting the dirt in your grocery bag. When you hit an artifact, note how deep it is in your bottle and draw where you found it at right. When you're done with your "dig," answer the following questions.

1. Which artifact is the oldest? How do you know?

_____

_____

2. Which artifact was most recently buried? How do you know?

_____

_____

3. Order your artifacts from oldest to the most recent.

Oldest: _____

_____

_____

_____

_____

Most Recent: _____

- **7 inches**

- **6 inches**

- **5 inches**

- **4 inches**

- **3 inches**

- **2 inches**

- **1 inch**

4. About an inch of new soil builds up on the ground each year. That means that something that fell on the ground 10 years ago is probably now covered by about 10 inches of soil. How old does that make each of your artifacts?

_____

_____

_____

Colonial America   Scholastic Professional Books

What Could It Be?

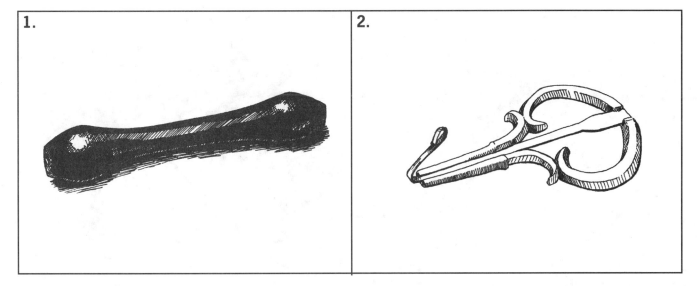

Look at the two colonial objects above. Now fill in the boxes below.
When you're done, check with your teacher to see how close to the
mark you were.

ARTIFACT	1	2
What is it made of?	clay	metal
Does it look like anything you know? What?		
What do you think it could have been used for? Why do you think this?		
What might it tell us about how colonists lived?		

Puzzling Evidence

**Cut out these pieces and then put them together on
another sheet of paper. Can you fill in what's missing?**

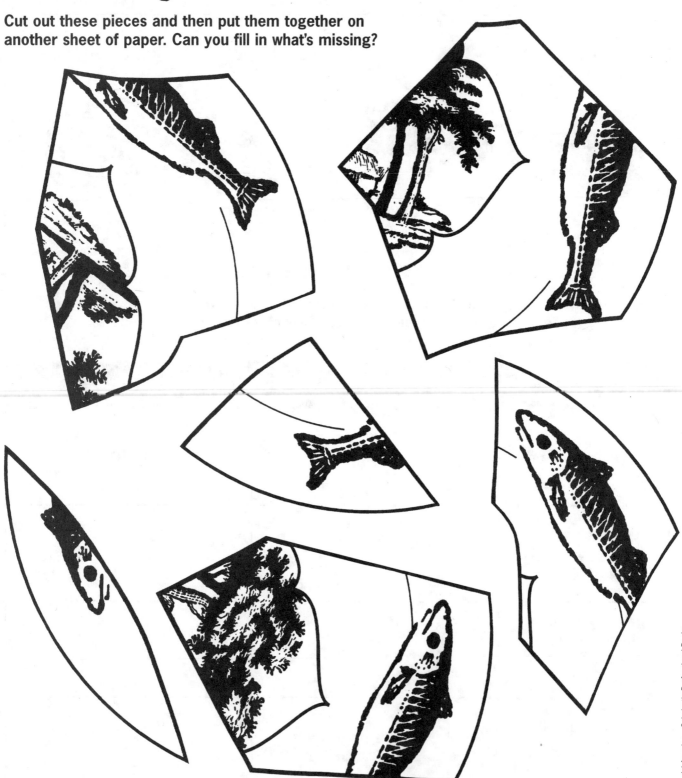

Colonial America   Scholastic Professional Books

Name _____

Hunting for History

What colonial person/place/thing am I researching? _____

When did he/she/it exist? _____

My person/place/thing is important because _____

_____

_____

_____

_____

Four fascinating facts about him/her/it are:

1. _____

_____

2. _____

_____

3. _____

_____

4. _____

_____

These resources helped me learn about my topic:

_____

_____

_____

_____

_____

_____

Classroom Resources

Books for Students

Introduce students to the different classes of colonial people with *A Williamsburg Household* by Joan Anderson (Clarion, 1988). It's a story about the very different lives of the gentry family and slave family who share and run a colonial household.

Another easy-to-read and information-packed book for students is *If You Grew Up With George Washington* by Ruth Belov Gross (Scholastic, 1982). It tells how Washington lived and learned in eighteenth-century Virginia.

The American Girl series, *Meet Felicity, a Colonial Girl, Felicity Learns a Lesson, Felicity's Surprise, Happy Birthday, Felicity!, Felicity Saves the Day*, and *Changes for Felicity* by Valerie Tripp (Pleasant Company, 1991–92) gives students a glimpse of colonial America.

Felicity's Cookbook: A Peek at Dining in the Past with Meals You Can Cook Today by Polly Athan (Pleasant Company Publications, 1994) is a colonial Virginia cookbook for young chefs. It's filled with easy-to-follow recipes for colonial foods, as well as information on how people cooked during colonial times.

Archaeology for Young Explorers by Patricia Samford and David L. Ribblett (The Colonial Williamsburg Foundation, 1995) is a great introduction—for both you and students—into how we search for the past. It's filled with interesting photographs, anecdotes about colonial Williamsburg, along with fun activities.

Colonial Life by Bobbie Kalman (Crabtree, 1992).

Slumps, Grunts, and Snickerdoodles: What Colonial America Ate and Why by Lila Perl (Seabury, 1975).

Williamsburg by Zachary Kent (Childrens Press, 1992).

Books for Teachers

An excellent teacher resource for information about all aspects of colonial life is John Warner's *Colonial American Home Life* (Franklin Watts, 1993).

USKids History: Book of the American Colonies by Howard Egger-Bovet (Little, Brown, 1996) is a rich resource book on colonial times and people. It covers the European exploration of North America from the Vikings to U.S. statehood through the eyes of historical characters. It includes games and activities.

John Anthony Scott's *Settlers on the Eastern Shore* (Facts on File, 1991) is another comprehensive sourcebook for teachers that describes how settlers struggled and prospered in the new colonies.

Other useful reference books include *George Washington's Rules of Civility & Decent Behavior* (Applewood Books, 1988) and *Daily Life, The Revolutionary War, The Explorers and Settlers, & Governing and Teaching* edited by Carter Smith (Millbrook Press, 1991). All are in the A Sourcebook on Colonial America series, part of the American Albums from the Collections of the Library of Congress.

Web Sites

- **http://www.colonialwilliamsburg.org/** Colonial Williamsburg's site includes a tour of the colonial town, loads of information on daily life and work—and even classroom-tested lesson plans! You shouldn't miss this one.

- **http://www.monticello.org/index.html** This fabulous site features information and fascinating facts about Thomas Jefferson and his life at Monticello.

- **http://www.plimoth.org/** For all you ever wanted to know about the Pilgrims and their home at Plymouth, check out this home page of Plimoth Plantation.

- **http://sln.fi.edu/franklin/rotten.html** You shouldn't miss this wonderful site on the world of Ben Franklin (which opens with his memorable aphorism, "If you would not be forgotten, as soon as you are dead and rotten, either write things worth reading, or do things worth the writing").

- **http://earlyamerica.com/** You may want to send advanced readers to this "Archiving Early America" site, which reconstructs life in revolutionary/post-revolutionary America through documents, newspapers, maps, and more.

- **http://www.mountvernon.org/** Want to know more about George Washington and his life at Mount Vernon? Check out the official Mount Vernon home page.

The Colonial Williamsburg Foundation offers a wide variety of books, teaching units, and audiovisual materials as well as reproductions of colonial toys, hats, games, and documents. For information, please call the John Greenhow Store, (757) 220-7536.

The Colonial Williamsburg Foundation also offers Electronic Field Trips, which are live interactive television programs that bring dramatic historical presentations and reenactments into the classroom. For more information, check out the Colonial Williamsburg Web site at **http://www.colonialwilliamsburg.org/**